WHAT PEOPLE ARE

THE WRITERS' GRC

You reap what you sow with writing groups, and Julie's book offers expert advice on how to sow effective seeds that will help a group flourish. She's scoured the world and interviewed writing groups in the UK, Europe, America and Australia to collate the best advice that every writing group – and member – should know. The Writing Group Handbook is essential reading for all writing groups, writing group members and anyone who is considering joining such a group.
Simon Whaley, Author of The Positively Productive Writer

A nice collection of advice, well-organized, and attentive to all the major topics that count.
Pam Nowak, RMFW, USA

I really enjoyed reading The Writers' Group Handbook and wished that it had been available when I started my first writing group, The Swanley Scribblers, fifteen years ago.

From the beginning, when the reader is asked to consider what they want from their group (and what sort of writer they wish to attend) through the psychology of potential members and onto workshop activities made me feel that I wanted to go out and look for another group straight away. I particularly enjoyed the section on common problems. Yes I could have done with that at one time too!

Written in a straightforward friendly way it will be a boon to anyone thinking of starting a writing group and indeed those already running a group, as this book gives food for thought for organisers and tutors alike.

The Writers' Handbook is an excellent and instructive read.

Well done to the author for writing such an informative guide.
Elaine Everest, Freelance Journalist

The Writers' Group Handbook by Julie Phillips is a useful resource tool to be recommended to writers wishing to get together and to take the plunge of forming themselves into a writing group. It contains all the information needed to move forward.
Pam Fish, Chair of The National Association of Writers' Groups

Compass Points

The Writers' Group Handbook

Compass Points

The Writers' Group Handbook

Julie Phillips

**COMPASS
BOOKS**

Winchester, UK
Washington, USA

First published by Compass Books, 2014
Compass Books is an imprint of John Hunt Publishing Ltd., Laurel House, Station Approach,
Alresford, Hants, SO24 9JH, UK
office1@jhpbooks.net
www.johnhuntpublishing.com
www.compass-books.net

For distributor details and how to order please visit the 'Ordering' section on our website.

Text copyright: Julie Phillips 2013

ISBN: 978 1 78279 138 6

A CIP catalogue record for this book is available from the British Library.

Design: Lee Nash

Printed and bound by CPI Group (UK) Ltd, Croydon, CR0 4YY

We operate a distinctive and ethical publishing philosophy in all
areas of our business, from our global network of authors to
production and worldwide distribution.

CONTENTS

Acknowledgements

I would like to thank all of the writing groups and experts who helped with this book, especially my own writing group Wrekin Writers, the 2012 retreaters and Simon Whaley, Di Perry, Bryan Vaughan, Darren Bailey, Brenda Carter, Suki White and Angeline Wheeler. They each brought their own unique wealth of experience and knowledge to show how good writing groups can be.

Thanks must also go to Pam Fish from NAWG and to Jonathan Telfer, editor of Writing Magazine, who was game enough to publish my thoughts on writing groups in the first place.

Introduction:
What A Writing Group Can Do For You

Why Form/Join A Writers' Group

As any writer knows, writing can be isolating. Spending hours hunched over your computer, typing your latest Work In Progress, can play havoc with your creativity. It's all too easy to become disengaged from the world around you and it can sometimes feel, after receiving rejections, that you are the only writer experiencing the disappointment rejections can bring.

But help is at hand if you want it. Joining a writers' group may seem daunting. You might even be in denial and not recognise yourself as the true writer you are.

"What will a writers' circle make of me?"

"I've not been published."

"I've only ever had a letter published in my local paper."

"They'll laugh me out of the room."

These are all negative things I've heard fellow writers say when I've asked if they belong to a writing group. There can be no room for such negativity!

It's no surprise so many writers are dubious about joining a writers' group when some groups are so dysfunctional it's a wonder they have any members left. I've heard tales of private feuds between members careering out of control, cliquey groups who are disparaging of any new members and groups that do the same boring read-a-round, meeting after meeting. You only get one life and sitting for an hour or two in a room full of blinkered, single minded, unhelpful writers is soul destroying and not conducive to creativity!

But, thankfully, most groups are fantastic, so don't be put off. Finding the right writers' group can be a challenge but not impossible. You need to try several on for size, fitness for purpose and comfort, as you would a new coat to get the right fit for you. There are no one-size fits all writing groups and no two writing groups will function in quite the same way.

I decided to join my local writing group, Wrekin Writers, www.wrekinwriters.co.uk, in 2008. I had just finished an Open University Creative Writing course and knew if left to my own devices I would struggle to find the motivation and inspiration to continue writing.

I also had little clue as how to progress my writing career. What I needed was a writing group to kick me into touch and keep me on the straight and narrow (as well as stop me from drowning in clichés!) But I have to confess that, at that time, I found the thought of walking into a room full of real, professional, experienced writers terrifying! I wasn't a real writer. I was just playing at it! I very nearly didn't make it through the door. I am so glad that I did as it kick started my professional writing career.

So, if you are a writer who is a member of a lacklustre writing group and you want to liven things up, or you are thinking of joining your local writing group but are unsure, or maybe you want to start your own writing group but have no idea where to start, this book is for you.

If you are a writer of any description, whether you are in a formal writing group or you just occasionally meet with writing friends, you will find lots of practical, motivational and inspirational advice here. With the knowledge and experience of a wealth of writers from a variety of writing groups across the UK, USA, Australia and Europe, you will find the answers to the many questions you have about writing groups.

Four years after I joined a writing group and several short stories, many articles, two blogs, an online short story critiquing blog, a column in one of the leading writing magazines in the UK, running several workshops, running an after-school creative writing club and now this book, I can say from experience that, for me, joining a writing group was the best thing I ever did for my writing career. Under their wings I was cajoled, encouraged, inspired, motivated, pushed and guided to be the writer I am today. Without their, quite frankly, bad influence, I doubt I would have ever found the self-confidence to even dare to send my writing out, let alone try to get anything published. And joining the right writers' group could be the best thing you ever do too.

Chapter One

What A Writer Wants

What Makes A Good Writers' Group?

If you are sitting at home, in a café or bar, lamenting your lonely life as a writer, you have probably received plenty of rejection slips to add to your wilting self-confidence. Oh, most of your family and friends will probably be supportive in the special way that only your closest friends and family can be. "That's nice, dear," they'll mutter, eyes still glued to their favourite TV programme. You have to remember that these are the same people who stuck your latest messy, sticky, early childhood attempts at art work on the fridge door every week. They are proud of you whatever you do.

But there can be no substitute for meeting with a group of like-minded, experienced writers who will tell it like it is. They will support you like your family but will tell you the bits you might not want to hear but should hear about your writing and how you can move forward with it. So what does a good writing group need?

Pam Fish, chair of the National Association of Writers' Groups, www.nawg.co.uk, says, "The group must have a dedicated leader. Because however much you try to get everyone involved and taking part there does need to be an 'organiser' to keep it all together, someone who will keep the continuity of the ideals of the group going. The group needs only to have a simple plan, but this plan needs to be kept to and unless there is someone to do this the group will likely fall apart."

Having your family and friends' support and attention, although important and nice, is not the same as having a roomful of professional, dedicated, know-what-they-are-talking-about writers who will study your writing in detail and give you the kind of constructive feedback you need. You won't hear any, "That's nice, dear," comments at a good writers' group meeting, or, at least, you shouldn't.

There is nothing better for gauging readers' reactions to your work as to reading it out loud in front of them, nerve wracking though it might be. Writers know writers. They understand what writers go through. They get you. Only another writer can understand why you spend hours typing away at your latest Work In Progress only to receive rejection after rejection, get up and dust yourself down and do it all again. Seemingly bashing your head against a brick wall is not the behaviour of a sane person!

When you join a writers' group you have the benefit of having access to a group of writers with the tools to help you to realise your writing goals. Writers' groups are a wonderful resource to tap into. You will find all kinds of writers there: professional, published writers, new writers, writers who write for pleasure and people who pretend they write but who just come along to the group for the social side or to publicise their cause. It takes all sorts to make a writing group and thank goodness for that! You will find a rainbow of colourful characters hanging out at a writers' group meeting who wouldn't be out of place in a novel! There is much inspiration to be had from simply observing your fellow writers.

So what makes a good writing group? The answer depends on what you want to get out of your writing group and what type of writing group you are looking for. I have spoken to people from many different writing groups and this is what some of them said that they wanted from a writing group:

"A mixed group of writers who meet regularly to share their work and try something new."
Louise Gibney, Towcester Writers' Group
www.misswrite.co.uk, towcesterwriters.weebly.com

"Members who are willing to share the knowledge they've acquired with all and wish each other well."
Janie Mason, Romance Writers of America, rwanational.org.

"A very informal group as I feel too many rules and regulations defeats the object of creative writing."
Maureen Blundell, Braintree Writers Group.

"A group where members feel quite at liberty to 'do their own thing', and indeed are encouraged by the others to write in their own way."
Toni Neville, U3A Weymouth & Portland.

"Groups should be welcoming."
Sharon Mignerey, founding member of Rocky Mountain Fiction Writers (RMFW), www.rmfw.org.

So, generally, a good writers' group will possess most of the following qualities:

Offer support and advice.
Offer varied workshops and speakers.
Offer good value for money.
Meet at a time and place convenient for most people wishing to join them.
Have members that are already professional writers and who have been published and who are willing to share their advice.
Provide somewhere they can share their work and have it appraised
Include a good balance of members: ages, personalities and people who write in different genres.
Are welcoming and encouraging.
Have an online presence members can go to between meetings.

Are not too big.

Are not too small.

Are well run and organised, with a clearly defined organiser.

Choosing The Right Group For You

Before searching for the right writers' group for you, spend some time writing down what it is that you want to gain from joining a group:

Do you want to be published? Or do you want to write for pleasure or attend more for the social/networking side of things?

Do you want a group which meets in the week in daytime? Or would you prefer a group which meets in an evening or at weekends?

Would you like to meet weekly or monthly?

Would a large group set your creativity tingling or make you hide behind your chair?

What age group of members would you like?

How much can you afford to spend on membership fees?

How far are you prepared to travel to get to meetings?

Do you want a highly structured group with set agendas each meeting or would you prefer a more relaxed approach?

Could you see yourself wanting to join the group's committee and helping out? Or do you want to just attend the meetings?

Do you want an all-female or all-male or a mixed group?

Do you want to offer up your work for scrutiny, read it out for members to give you constructive feedback? Or do you want to listen to others' work, have workshops on how to write or a mixture?

"A writer should look for a group that focuses on helping writers develop their craft rather than tearing them down.

Look at the purpose of the group and its reputation. Visit a few events or meetings to see if you like the feel of the group." Pamela Nowak, Rocky Mountain Fiction Writers, USA.

Once you have decided your requirements you can then surf the internet, enquire at your local library, ask your local council, community centre or College of Further Education for information on writers' groups in your area and look at their websites to see if any match your needs. Looking on the National Association of Writers' Group Website at their Writers' Groups directory would also be a good idea. www.nawg.co.uk

Try Before You Buy

Most writers' groups have a 'try before you buy' system where your first session is free. Don't be shy about trying a few out before you commit either. Joining a writing group is a big step for most writers, especially those new to writing, and you don't want to be put off by a writing group that doesn't meet your needs. As writer, editor and photographer Penny Legg, who set up her own writing group, Writing Buddies, pennyleggswriting-buddies. blogspot.com, in 2009 says:

"Author Simon Whaley once gave me a very good piece of advice. He knew I was looking for a writing group to join. He told me that you have to try on writing groups to find out which one fits. I did not quite understand what he meant until I went along to a couple of writing groups and found that I did not fit in. I then understood. Having found what I did not want, it was easier to say what I did want from any group I attended."

It is only by trying a few different writing groups that you will find one that suits you and makes you feel that you are among like-minded friends who just want to write and grow as writers.

Joining a writers' group is a big decision, so don't rush it.

Louise Gibney, founder of Towcester Writers' Group, says: "I have been to meetings in four other groups. It's great to get an idea of what other groups are doing and how they run their groups, but I eventually chose the group that was closest to me at that time."

What To Avoid

I know of writers who have had bad experiences with writers' groups and were put off trying other groups out. This is a real shame as most writers' groups are lively, dynamic and listen to what their members want and do their utmost to deliver that. But what if there is a fly in the ointment of your writing group? What can you do to stop it happening in the first place?

Be clear about your writing group's mission statement: who is your writing group for? What does it want to achieve?

Keep order: Make sure members are aware regarding the running order of the meetings and expectations of behaviour during the meeting.

Lighten up: having too formal a group might put off potential members who are excellent writers and could offer a lot to the group.

Don't get drawn into personal feuds and personality clashes within the group, but don't put up with them either.

Don't take it personally: there will always be moans and groans in any group.

Don't do it all yourself: you might sometimes feel that it would be quicker, more efficient and of better quality if you did it yourself, but if you take on more than you can cope with the group will suffer. It's important to get a good team working alongside you: a good organiser, someone who is fabulous with figures, a people person and you'll be set.

Be tactful: probably one of the most important traits to have if you're leading a writing group!

Smile! It will get better with time and experience.

Chapter Two

Right From The Start

Setting Up Your Own Writing Group

The first question you need to ask yourself, if you are thinking of setting up your own writing group is, "Do I have the time, resources and money to commit to it?" Starting your own writing group, although exciting and inspiring, is a huge commitment and the buck will always stop with you. Not that I am trying to put you off! Far from it. Running your own group can be challenging, but rewarding too. You just need to make sure that your plans for the group are meticulously thought out and that you get as much help as you can.

The Three 'P's

The three **P's** are important here: Preparation, Persistence and Production.

Preparation: This is your master plan. You need to sit down and write down everything you want the group to be, source potential venues, times/dates of meetings, fees, advertising, names of people who might be able to help you, council or Government assistance, media, etc. Be prepared to be flexible with it. You will need to change some things and make compromises.

Persistence: Rome wasn't built in a day and neither will your writing group. You might find yourself banging your head against a brick wall many times. Your task is to vary the head banging technique until you cause small cracks to appear in the wall and it begins to crumble. Keep going with your idea and it will grow, eventually.

Production: Think of your writing group as a musical. You are the director, but a Broadway smash a director alone does not make! You need actors, make up, costumes, lighting, scripts, choreography, prompts, etc., to make the show a success. You have to produce an enticing and fit for purpose writing group but you can't produce an all singing, all dancing writing group alone, even though it might feel like you are doing the lion's share of the work most of the time. If you burn out before you've hit the ground running, a writing group you won't have!

The Six 'W's

Above all, when you are planning your writing group, it will help if you can answer the following six questions: What? When? Where? Who? Why? How?

What will be your group's ethos? What are you trying to achieve with your group?

When will you meet?

Where will you meet?

Who are your target potential members? Age, gender, type of writer, published or non-published, writing for pleasure, writing for therapy, a mixture?

Why do you want to set it up? Is there really a need for a new writing group in your area?

How are you going to pull all the strands together and make it work?

Anyone who enjoys writing would be well advised to join their local writing group. They can provide support, expertise and a place to meet other writers. But what if there isn't a writing group near to you? Or, what if you've tried the ones that are available and found they are not for you? It could be time to consider setting up your own writing group. Is it as hard as it might at first appear?

Penny Legg, founder of Writing Buddies. based in Southampton, says: "It is not as difficult as you may think! There are a lot of writers, or would-be writers, who welcome the chance to get out of the family circle, where everything they write is 'super', and mix with other writers at the same or a different place in their writing career. This opens horizons."

You might find that there are people out there just waiting for the right writing group to come along and why shouldn't it be the one that you set up? Penny's experience of setting up her own writing group proves it can be done. But how can you make the process of organising such a group easier?

"Have an idea what you want your group to achieve," Penny suggests.

Having an idea of the ethos and philosophy of your group will go a long way to help you setting one up. But is there anyone out there who can help you.

Pam Fish, chair of NAWG, states that they are only too happy to help fledgling groups along. "By joining NAWG you will have the support of many like-minded people; have a copy of their bi-monthly magazine LINK which, as well as keeping you informed about other members and writing groups, gives you the opportunity to be published. NAWG have a very informative website which lists open competitions and other activities available to writers, all in one place."

"Keep things simple," Penny adds. "The more rules and regulations, bureaucracy and red tape you have, the harder it is to run and be realistic about the time you can spend with the group."

Are there any pitfalls?

Tony Gutteridge, treasurer of Grace Dieu Writers' Circle, www.gracedieuwriterscircle.co.uk, based in Leicester, says: "I think there is always the danger of recruiting overly officious people to the Steering Group. Our Steering Group has worked best when populated with moderate people. I also think it important that the whole writing group knows what it is about."

Starting off small then building on the group's success means you can iron out any teething problems and keep things manageable.

Author and photographer Simon Whaley, www.simon-whaley.co.uk, adds: "I would seriously consider creating a constitution. It's simply a list of rules about how the group will operate. Ask another group for a copy of theirs that you can adapt for your own group."

Have a look at Wrekin Writers' constitution as a template to start you off. www.wrekinwriters.co.uk.

It takes careful and considered organisation to start your own writing group. But it's been done many times before so don't be afraid to give it a go as there is help out there from NAWG and other writing groups as well as your local council and library to help you on your way. It could be the solution if you're struggling to find a suitable writing group in your location.

The other thing to consider is how big a committee you want and which roles you need to fulfil. Depending on the size of your group, the basic triangle of a chairperson, treasurer and secretary will be enough to start you off. You need someone who is good at organising and managing people at the helm as chair person, someone good with figures to keep the group's finances in order and a secretary to help with communications.

What advice does Tony Gutteridge have on forming a committee? "A writing group does need some direction and I believe it important to have a group of people to lead on this. The Steering Group decides on certain things, e.g. the annual programme of assignments."

But how do you decide who takes on these roles within the group's committee? Tony suggests: "It is hard to get people to sit on committees, so we look for volunteers. If we have no volunteers, we cajole people to sit on the Steering Group. At one time we used to hold elections to recruit Steering Group members, but this was rare."

Generally, in groups where elections are held, members are asked to nominate themselves or other members to stand for the roles on offer. If there is only one nominee then this is fairly straightforward. If there is more than one, ask those nominees interested in the same role to give a short speech on why they think they can do the role and ask them to leave the room while a secret ballot is conducted. The person with the most votes wins. Holding this ballot yearly, at the group's Annual General Meeting, is ideal as members can have the chance to become the chairperson or any other role they like.

But Tony warns: "Keep it fairly informal and don't get wrapped up in formality. Writing groups are there for people's enjoyment so shouldn't emulate work!"

Some roles are essential but others might not yet be appropriate for your group. They include:

Chairperson: is the group leader in overall charge of the group. This role is important as he or she oversees the smooth running of the group. **Vice Chair:** not essential but can help to shoulder some of the responsibility with the Chairperson. A problem shared is a problem halved!

Secretary: takes care of all communications and keeps paperwork in order.

Treasurer: keeps financial records and produces an annual treasurer's report to the group.

Publicity/Liaison Officer: works on publicising the group and engaging speakers and activities for the group.

Competition Secretary: responsible for collating all competition entries and distributing them to the judges as well as producing a list of shortlisted stories and winners. They will also notify winners.

Webmaster: responsible for setting up and running/updating the group's website as well as social networking and keeping members informed of any relevant material passed through the website and e-mail address.

Mark Stevens, President of Rocky Mountain Fiction Writers (RMFW), says, "Our board has 17 members but, under our by-laws, the key individuals are the president, vice-president, treasurer, secretary and published author liaison representative. Those five are the executive committee and conduct the business end of the operation."

Pam Nowak, also of RMFW, adds, "By-laws should be drafted to establish the mission of the group and its organisation. Policies and procedures should be added to detail how the mission will be accomplished. The policies and procedures will ensure that the group will be run consistently."

Tony continues, "The website administrator needs to be familiar with computers, but huge technical skills aren't vital as the website software we use is designed for the non-expert. The other main skills needed by all Steering Group members are in the areas of communications and organisation.

"Grace Dieu is quite an informal group (we like it that way). None of the Steering Group has formal roles, apart from the treasurer and the website administrator. At Steering Group meetings, we discuss the issues of the day, mainly to do with our ongoing programme of meetings, events, our internal competition, etc. Depending on what we plan, different members of the Steering Group will take responsibility for specific activities, but will have support from the other members."

Money Matters

It is also worth setting up a group bank account; all major banks will allow you to do this. For the minimal inconvenience of filling in a few forms, keeping a simple balance sheet of income and expenditure is all you need.

Bryan Vaughan, www.bryanvaughan.co.uk, treasurer for Wrekin Writers based in Shropshire, explains, "We have a petty cash box for raffle money and prize money for chairman's challenges, a bank account for annual subscriptions, paying for room hire and speakers, and a Paypal account for entries to our short story competition. Of course many people still send cheques as the entry fee, so a bank account is important for those too.

"Managing the group's finances is not difficult, but it does demand some dedication to record the movement of money. I inherited the role of treasurer along with a folder and paper records for petty cash and bank account transactions. After a couple of years I started to use a computer spreadsheet instead, which meant I could easily track where the money was coming from and going to (subscriptions, room hire, external speaker fees, competition entries, etc.) It also made it easier to run the final year report to tell the group how their subscriptions were spent, and to share the information with the group. I keep a backup of course."

Keeping records, especially financial ones, is important for the smooth running of the group. You need to be able to prove on a written basis all of your incomings and outgoings so that everything is kept above board and there can be no accusations of impropriety. It protects you as leader of the group as well as all your members.

Bryan suggests, "A bank account is important to keep things

clear and unambiguous, legally and financially. We have a Clubs and Societies account, which is ideal for organisations with a small turnover. It's free to use and has no charges for transactions or paying in cheques. It comes with a chequebook to make payments and online banking is available.

"It's recommended to set up the bank account to require 2 or more signatures to authorise cheques or make changes, such as loan agreements. We have 3 authorised signatories, but only 2 are needed, which gives some flexibility in case someone is away.

"Paypal (www.paypal.com) is a popular online payment service, which can be linked with your bank account and make or receive payments. There is a small charge to receive payments, but the convenience of not having to take cheques to the bank is often worth it."

Taxing Times

The only things that are inevitable in life are paying taxes and death! But does working out your group's tax affairs have to be a fate worse than death? No, says Bryan Vaughan (thankfully!).

"As an unincorporated club, we are liable for Corporation Tax on our profits. Profit is defined as what is left of your income for the year after all your tax allowances are deducted. These are all the costs you incur in order to run your club, and include room hire, bank or Paypal charges, speaker hire and prize money. Only if your profit exceeds the corporation tax threshold do you then pay tax on the excess. We pretty much break even every year, so our tax obligation is nothing. Most small clubs run for the benefit of their members will be the same, and HM Revenue and Customs treat them as 'dormant' for the purposes of corporation tax, and do not send out reminder letters to file taxes."

Is it the same in the USA?

"By-laws allow a group to apply for particular recognition and tax status, depending upon the mission (non-profit, service, or educational, for example)," Pam Nowak advises.

Janie Mason of RWA adds: "We have a website, cofw.org, as well as a Facebook page and a members' Yahoo loop. Due to our non-profit status with the Internal Revenue Service of the United States, we cannot use these outlets for self-promotion. They are to promote the chapter as a whole, to inform and educate members and to share our writing successes."

Something to be aware of when looking at legitimate ways to advertise your group and raise funds without falling foul of the tax office.

"More information on taxation is available from www.hmrc. gov.uk or, for the USA, www.irs.gov."

Once your membership grows it will also be worthwhile creating a simple database with your members' names and contact details. This will make it easier to see the size and variety of your membership as well as keeping tabs on who has paid and who hasn't.

As well as how much you are going to charge, another important factor is whether members should pay monthly or yearly. You can have different members doing both but it might be easier and more economical to have a flat rate yearly rate which is calibrated on a sliding scale dependent on which month any member joins. But it's important to give members the choice; they may lose out if they are only able to attend 7 out of the 12 meetings but have paid for the year. Be flexible.

Writer and blogger, Morgen Bailey, morgenbailey.wordpress. com, suggests that, from a financial point of view, "There could be grants groups can obtain from their local council, the National Arts Council or maybe even from the government (www.govern-mentfunding.org.uk/page.aspx?SP=245)."

It's always worth making enquiries with your local council and library as to whether any money is available, particularly start-up funds. If you don't ask, you don't get.

Once the group is more established, it could explore other avenues to make money for itself, as in:

Delivering reasonable cost workshops to other writing groups or other groups and societies in the community.

Increasing members' subs.

Putting together an anthology of members' work and selling it.

Selling refreshments in the break at meetings.

Morgen Bailey also suggests, "The first thing is to look at the writing group's biggest expenses; likely to be room hire. Do they need the size of room they have? Can they downgrade or better still, will one of the members be willing to hold the meetings at their house, or alternating?"

Forming a committee is one of the first most important jobs your writing group should do. Once the committee is in place it can drive the group forward and keep the group's finances in check. Knowing you have an excellent team of enthusiastic, knowledgeable, experienced and hard-working people who share your passion for writing and the group working with you takes the pressure off and makes the running of the group a whole lot easier.

What's In A Name?

When you've considered the basics of where and when you're going to meet and what your committee will look like, the next important step is to consider an appropriate name. This is not as simple as you think. You could go down one of several routes before making your decision:

Geographical – gives potential members an idea of the area in which your group is based.

Themed – lets people know the genre in which you write, i.e. poetry, novels etc.

Eye-catching – something completely different that will set you apart from other writing groups and gain attention.

Traditional – named after a member who is no longer with you or a famous writer from your area.

Rita Elliott from Seriously Sentences writing group based in Wales, gladstoneslibrary.org/writinggroup/, says that her writing group's name followed a tradition of other groups that share the same meeting place – a reading group called Seriously Books and a film group called Seriously Film.

Rita says: "I suppose Seriously Sentences, backed up with the Gladstones' library logo makes it sound as though we are looking for serious writers. There are many members of the group who are actively seeking publication."

Will a quirky name get you more attention than a name based on where the group meets?

Mary Ellen Foley, chair of Hog's Back Writers, www.hogsback writers.org.uk, based in Surrey, says: "A name should help the members themselves to feel that they are real writers (whatever that means to them), and it should say something about what kind of writers they are or want to be. The name shouldn't give the wrong impression, and shouldn't seem to limit the possibilities for the group."

In any business, the company name and logo are key to projecting the right image for that company. The right name and logo can make millions and set the company apart and ahead of its competitors – so you can understand why companies spend so much time and money on the graphic design and marketing of their company's brand.

Mary Ellen offers: "As for the importance of the name, I'm of two minds. The name has to suit on at least two levels: how it makes the members feel about the group, and what kind of image the name presents to non-members."

"I don't know where the Hog's Back Writers sit on this scale, but it does seem to me that if the name projects amateurism, the writers involved will think of themselves and their work differently."

Rita Elliot thinks that a writing group should not lose sleep over choosing a name. "How important is the name? I'm not sure it really matters. What's been delightful about Seriously Sentences so far is not the label or the concept of a writing group, it's the individuals who had the courage to sign up and develop their writing."

Whatever you choose to call your group, remember it's the attitude and imagination of the group itself that is important and not just the packaging. When it comes to gaining new members or publicising your group's work, it's the atmosphere and enthusiasm within the group that really counts.

Chapter Three

Entertaining The Troops

Getting To Know You

Writing group meetings can be hectic. By the time you've got through the initial agenda covering issues like writing successes, members' news, future plans and the rest of it, you're on to the workshop or read around. Sometimes you can hardly draw breath before you're on to the next item. It can be exhausting and leave members feeling like they are being dragged behind a fast car, unaware of who is at the wheel and who the fellow passengers are. Maybe it's time to take your foot off the gas and park up for a while.

It's a little easier in smaller groups where everyone knows pretty much everyone else, but in a larger group it can be difficult to keep tabs on who is who and, if you don't build socialising or 'free' time into the schedule, you may find your group in danger of forming little cliques where never the twain shall meet.

Maureen Blundell, who writes as Roz Colyer, belongs to Braintree Writers who have been meeting for four years and value the importance of socialising. "We meet once a fortnight in the evening in a local pub. We are a very informal group as I feel too many rules and regulations defeat the object of creative writing."

Meeting in small groups, like Braintree Writers, in a place like the pub where it is easier to chat, can be the solution to getting to know each member better. But if you're a larger group which can't meet in the evening, or have difficulty finding suitable venues because of the sheer size of the group, it can be hard to socialise.

Pam Fish, chair of NAWG, advises holding social events to

aid members in their quest to get to know each other. "Encourage members to bring their other half. Maybe this should be done on another occasion from the main group meeting – an afternoon or evening, or a day out. Make this event a something-for-everyone evening. Groups could meet in a local park for a game of cricket and a picnic. And then, as always, write about it afterwards, for a writing exercise at a meeting."

This is exactly what Braintree Writers did. "We have trips to theatres and outings to Hedingham Castle for the annual Shakespeare play by the Globe touring company," says Maureen Blundell. "Some members of the group also write, produce and perform plays for a local hospital radio."

It's good for groups to relax and let their hair down for a while. Going heavy on the writing agenda can become tiresome and instead of motivating and inspiring it has the opposite effect. Finding an activity or day out that has wide appeal is the key to getting the socialising ball rolling as Braintree Writers have discovered.

Other groups, such as Wrekin Writers from Shropshire, who have a 30 plus membership, have a refreshment break midway in the meeting where members can convene in a café area and relax with a coffee and biscuits for an informal chat before the workshop starts. This valuable time allows members to sit next to other members they might not have had the chance to chat to before – everyone feels included and valued (and refreshed).

If groups are finding it hard to connect, Maureen has this advice: "Writers usually have interests in common and specialise in short stories, novels or poetry, so possibly splinter groups catering for these specific areas might be an idea if the group itself is big enough. It's important to realise what each individual member of the group needs from the group and to cater for them appropriately."

Sitting down together and doing something unrelated to writing away from regular group meetings could be the way forward if your writing group doesn't connect. It takes time to build friendships and relationships and writing groups are not immune from this.

For a bit of fun, encourage members to sit in different parts of the room at each meeting – this could be done by members picking a random seat number out of a hat.

Have a different 'meeter' and 'greeter' every meeting to welcome new members and look after the newer recruits.

Have a rota of social events outside of regular meetings so members have the chance to circulate and have fun.

Play 'creeping death,' an ice breaker where every member has the opportunity to say a little bit about themselves at the start of the meetings.

Don't force the issue – let members get to know each other at their own pace.

Keeping Your Members Happy

So, you've set up your brand new, squeaky clean writing group. You are full of grand plans and enthusiasm for the group and have a good idea of where you want your group to be. From humble beginnings, with a handful of members, you know you have a long way to go and have some idea of what you want to achieve. But how are you going to keep your precious members motivated to attend each meeting? You have to grab their attention and hold it.

The key here is to canvass your members to find out what it is they hope to get out of the group as it may be far removed from your vision! You can do this as a very informal meeting down the pub way, or a more formal questionnaire can be handed out at the next meeting. More simply, you could just ask members during the meeting; whichever way suits you and your members.

Some people prefer a more anonymous approach and do not

like speaking out in group settings, whilst others are only too happy to voice their opinions out in the open forum. Giving your members options will make them feel part of the group and that they have a say in the way the group is run. Giving them ownership and some responsibility will make them feel included and more likely to keep pitching up each meeting.

Angie Hodapp, RMFW Program Chair, advises, "Variety is key to keeping members' attention, but it's crucial to keep programming focussed on the organisation's mission too."

A happy member is a returning member and there's nothing like having happy, positive members spreading the good word about your group! But how do you go about giving your members what they want from their writing group when they are all very different people with very different, and often opposing, views and needs?

If you want your writing group to be an environment of encouragement, motivation, inspiration and a hot bed for helping its members to reach their full writing potential then you are going to have to listen to their opinions. Then you can work them into a programme of writing events that works for most of your members most of the time.

You Can't Please Everyone All The Time!

It's impossible to please everyone all of the time and a writing group environment is testament to this! If you try to please everyone you will fail, so don't waste your efforts and risk a headache by trying to. It would be better to take note of what your members said when you canvassed them, get your committee together one evening over a drink and come up with a workable programme for your meetings that addresses all of the main issues that concern writers of all genres.

That is not to say that you have to be bland and generic. There's no reason why you cannot concentrate on one theme per meeting with the premise that you will get round to many of the themes members suggested. It might be a good idea to give members a copy of the proposed programme so they can comment on it, and if there's a workshop or writing event there they have no interest in they have the option of giving that a miss but attending the one after which is pertinent to them.

Common themes that most writing group members will be interested in are listed below, although this list is not by any means complete as, by their very natures, all writers are different as are all writing groups.

Grammar
How to write short stories
How to write novels
How to write articles
Self-publishing
How to present your work to an editor/publisher
Poetry workshops
How to pitch an idea to an editor
Travel writing
Writing romance/horror/fantasy/erotica/thriller/crime/any
genre you can think of
Using your senses in your writing
Finding rhythm in your writing

Remember that you don't have to do it all yourself. Encourage your committee and members to do some work too. You are not the only writer in your group! There should be plenty of ideas floating around in the ether of your members' creative minds! If there's something they'd like to have covered or can cover themselves, then great. You can save a lot of time and money by getting your members involved in planning and executing workshops.

Your Flexible Friend

One thing to avoid is getting your writing group into a rut. We've probably all been there. There's a read around of work for the fourth meeting in a row; the chairperson is snoozing in the corner and several members have drool pooling on the table in front of them, their eyes glazed over in a trance of boredom. If you're trying to retain members and gain more, this shabby, uninspiring group meeting format is not going to cut it.

Yes, you need a programme of events for your group and outline how each meeting is to be run, but don't let it be set in stone. Flexibility is your friend here so use it to its fullest advantage. There are certain things in any group that have to be tackled but you don't have to do them in the same order all of the time!

Shaking the agenda up every now and then will not only wake your poor, bored members up, it will keep things fresh which can only be good for your group's creativity. Making the extraordinary out of the ordinary will keep your members' attention far more than the usual bog standard chalk and talk. So think about how you can present the information for your workshops to your group. A little lateral thinking and ingenuity spicing up your workshops will be memorable for all the right reasons.

A variety of speakers talking about a variety of subjects could certainly help satisfy most members' needs, but does it always have to be about writing? Pam Fish, chair of NAWG, doesn't think so. "Introduce social events: fish and chip supper? Cupcake competition? Themed evening (Spanish, French,) My idea here is to get members talking about things other than writing, because in the long run this will make members more interested in what is going on. Encourage members to arrange one of these events for the rest of the group.

"These should only be occasional events but always keep them on the agenda and then invite members to write about it. If the group can afford it, arrange for a professional writer to give a talk. If the group can't afford to do this for themselves, make it an open event, welcome the public and invite another group to do it with you."

The idea is to bring an element of surprise into the meetings, to bring something new to the table to help stave off the boredom and give members the chance to participate in something they wouldn't usually have the opportunity to. This could be the breeding ground for new writing ideas.

Tony Gutteridge, treasurer and organiser of Grace Dieu writers based in Leicester, says: "The group is here because of its interest in writing, so all of our workshops have a writing theme, although not always about the techniques of writing. Twice a year we have social events so we do ring some non-writing stuff into the calendar."

Recruiting New Members

It is likely, when you first set up your group, that you will be small but enthusiastic. This is not a problem. In fact, starting off small and simple is often the best way. It takes time, patience and a lot of hard work to build up a good writing group, so take your time when planning it.

Writers are strange creatures and it can be isolating to be cooped up in our writing spaces for hours with strong coffee and a secret stash of chocolate our only companions and comforts. So for a writer to prise themselves away from their little castle to attend a writing group meeting is often a big step and they will expect something special for their efforts, otherwise you probably won't see them again.

Your existing members are your greatest tools in increasing your membership. Provide your members with a dynamic and forward reaching programme and you're half way there. Their opinion on the group and enjoyment of it will be what pulls in other members. What you want is for your members to leave each meeting floating on cloud nine, full of fizz for their next writing project. Believe me, this attitude and experience is highly contagious! I've lost count of the times I've walked into one of my writing group meetings feeling deflated and dejected but left with a spring in my step and an inspired mind ready to roll with my writing again. A writing group's influence is powerful: they make you believe that you can write so therefore you can write!

Planning alternative activities for your group should involve the opinions of all your members. Having a policy of 'all suggestions gratefully received' will give your members ownership of their group and provide an atmosphere of creativity and inspiration for all members so that they want to contribute to the group, therefore getting out of it what they want but also putting back in what they can.

Read All About It!

You could advertise your group in a variety of settings. The chairman of Wrekin Writers places a small advert in the local paper in the Community Lines which runs every few weeks and the group have gained members this way.

Simon Whaley, author and photographer and one time chairman of Wrekin Writers, suggests this to help publicise your group: "When you've decided on a date and a venue, give yourself plenty of time to publicise your first meeting. Send a press release to your local paper and give a contact number so that prospective members can ring you first to chat about what you're hoping to achieve. It's an opportunity to sell your group. Ask the local library to put posters up on their notice boards and use any community notice boards in your area to publicise the event. Can you get a mention on local radio? Many have community group slots where they can advertise events and meetings."

Getting your group a website is also an option, although a blog hosted by WordPress or Blogger, for example, and social networking pages such as Facebook or Myspace, will be equally as good to start with. You can reach an immense audience for free in this way, give information about forthcoming events and meetings and where you meet and how often. Details of how your group operates can be helpful. We will look at the issues around gaining your group an online presence in Chapter 9.

Workshops

You don't have to go to any great expense here. Often the simplest are the best. If your writing group is just starting out or if you are on a low budget, it might be wise to have members of your own group to step in and do a workshop or two. A few members of my own writing group have done just this and it works well. But when you're up and running, and especially if you want more members and keep your existing members' attention, you will need to branch out and source speakers from outside.

Morgen Bailey says, "Many local published authors are willing to give a talk for free in the hope that they may sell some of their books. Workshops are another great way of building on the knowledge base of the group and can be a reasonable cost if the tutors are local."

Angie Hodapp, RMFW, also goes down the local line. "We hold free monthly workshops. Presenters are local folks who either volunteer to teach a topic of their choice or whom we invite to teach a particular topic. Twice a year we hold all-day education events with a highly respected industry professional, an agent, editor or author."

Having your own members do workshops is all well and good but it can become a little boring. By occasionally offering your group workshops by a writer or other such person who is not well known to the group, you will spark their imagination and attention by virtue of it being someone new and, hopefully, who has been published or is successful in some other way.

You may have noticed that I used the phrase 'or other such person' earlier. By this I mean that your workshops do not have to be and should not be all about writing. It does a writing group good to veer off the beaten writing track and take a journey along the road less travelled.

For instance, I have done a workshop where I encouraged my writing group members to rediscover their inner child and find inspiration for their writing through child's play. It's almost impossible to ignore Lego and Play Doh. And it's irresistible to place your hand in a tub of cold spaghetti or jelly, whilst blind folded, and try to describe what it feels like!

Another workshop undertaken by Simon Whaley involved a mixing bowl and a recipe for writing. A further one involved a whisk that wasn't really a whisk. Oh no, it was a beacon for aliens trying to locate Earth and land their craft. It was a television or radio receiver, an outlandish earring – something you wouldn't ordinarily associate with the spark for a story! And have you ever had members parading around your meetings dressed as a punctuation mark to help explain grammar? Wrekin Writers have!

We once had a drumming workshop too, as far removed from writing or a read around as you can imagine. Or was it? We certainly all found our inner drummer and our inner rhythm that meeting which soon vibrated its way into our writing.

We also had author and motivational speaker, Liam O'Connell, www.liamoconnell.co.uk in, against the better judgement of some members who were unsure as to how he would help them. Some of them, me included, were so glad they attended that particular workshop, I can tell you. He was one of the best speakers we've ever had and he had such a profound effect on many of us, myself in particular. His influence is still resonating with the group today.

All writing and no play makes a writer (and their writing) very dull indeed. Allowing your writing group to let their hair down once in a while and experience something completely different will do them (and their writing) a world of good.

So how do you go about finding an outside speaker for your group?

Ask your members. Do they have a buddy, cousin, aunt, acquaintance or work colleague who could do a star turn? Your members are your first port of call and a mine of information/ contacts.

Search the internet for local authors, writers, photographers and anyone else you feel might be of interest to the group.

Advertise on your website/social media page for people willing to come and do a workshop.

Are there any writing groups near you who might be willing to do an exchange? They send someone from their group to you to do a workshop and vice versa.

Word of mouth: does anyone have any recommendations for someone who might agree to do a workshop?

Ask the editors of local publications to come down. They are often a good port of call with some interesting insights into the world of publishing and priceless information for budding writers.

Get Out More: Trips And Retreats

Everyone knows that a change is as good as a rest, so why don't you and your writing group go on a trip? Getting away from it all and your usual meeting place can work wonders for your creativity and motivation levels. You don't have to go far. Even if you are just meeting in a different location, it can be enough to let the inspiration explode.

Another way of getting out and about is to go for a weekend retreat. If you can't commit to a weekend away, then why not consider a day trip? Places of historical interest are popular here as are local landmarks and places of literary interest.

You don't have to go to great expense or go far, but a change of scenery will do your writing group's writing a power of good as well as break up the usual meeting format and prevent it all from becoming stale.

The main points to consider when planning to go away are:

Where do you want to go?

What time of year do you want to go? Certain times of the year will be cheaper and more available than others.

For how long? A morning, afternoon, day or weekend?

What will be your travelling arrangements?

How much will it cost?

Who will organise it and how?

Where will you eat/drink? Packed lunch, self-catering or pub lunch?

How many will be going?

How will it be paid for? Will members pay a fee or will it come out of subs?

Planning an outing or retreat doesn't have to be taxing or headache inducing as long as it's well organised and members know what to expect. Starting off small is the key thing to remember here. Arranging to hold one meeting in a different venue will do to begin with. Then, as you become more confident and feel like experimenting and being more adventurous, arranging a trip for a couple of hours to a local tourist attraction, perhaps, will work well.

Once your group has been going for some time and have got to know each other better, a day trip further away from base might fit the bill followed by a weekend retreat. Wrekin Writers, based in Shropshire, have held an annual retreat for the past few years. Because we are based close to Wales, our retreat venues are in various locations within Wales. Getting 12 retreaters organised is not for the faint hearted but is not impossible, as long as a sub-group of members are roused to organise it. It's too much work for one person to deal with.

Once you have an idea of how many of your members are interested, you can begin to search for suitable places. I would advise that you keep the numbers to below ten for your first retreat as you are more likely to find a place big enough to accommodate you all and it will be far easier to manage. A quick search on the Internet will throw up a list of potential venues which you can then contact regarding availability and cost.

A word of warning, however: make sure you get a deposit from members who wish to attend before you book, unless you are prepared to make a loss when some members pull out or don't pay their deposit. Then give members a deadline for paying their deposit on the understanding that if they don't pay they don't go. It may sound harsh and authoritarian, but, trust me; you don't want to be landed with a big bill because some members have pulled out. Having a written rule that the deposit is non-refundable might also help. It might sound mean, but it's not funny when you have to pay more each because someone drops out. £1000/$500 divided by ten members is a lot less than if three drop out and you end up dividing it between seven of you.

Remember that a retreat is not only a way to get to know each other, it's your group members' chance to get away from real life for a while and live life as they imagine they would should they have the opportunity to be a full-time writer. If you are always bemoaning your lack of writing time, you will have it in abundance on a retreat, with the added bonus of sharing time with like-minded writers. Do not underestimate the power of other writers' influence on your flagging motivation and inspiration levels. The experiences you have whilst on retreat will carry you on long after you have returned home.

Organising a short trip away or a long weekend retreat has to consider all members' needs and interests in order for the group to connect and fully engage in and enjoy the trip. They won't get much out of it if their needs are neglected.

It also helps, when trying to gel the group together, if all members attending the retreat are assigned a responsibility too. Suggestions you might like to consider are:

An astute and bargain hunting shopper to organise food and provisions (doing it all online can be a time saver as long as they deliver to your retreat venue).

A good negotiator and people person to book the place and act as liaison between the owners of the venue and the group.

Someone to collect the money and deal with the finances of the retreat.

A good cook and menu planner to plan and cook meals/ organise sandwiches and pub meals, etc.

Someone to organise transport. Car sharing works well here.

A rota drawn up before you go should prevent any disagreements whilst on retreat so that everyone knows what their roles are. It's neither fair nor fun if you are the one doing the lion's share of the work. Remember it's supposed to be a retreat for everyone.

It's also a good idea to discuss with your group what members want from the day trip or retreat before you go. Do they want an organised tour or time to wander by themselves? Do they want to have planned workshops whilst on retreat or find their own writing nook and be left to their own devices, meeting up as a whole group for an evening meal?

Making sure that all members are aware of and have agreed to the plan will make your job and the retreat a whole lot easier. But, again, remember that flexibility is your friend here. Even with the best laid plans things can and do go wrong: a member's SatNav will malfunction, leaving them in the middle of nowhere; there will inevitably be no mobile phone signal; another member's car will break down; the shopping will not be delivered until after many anxious phone calls.

Making sure that you have a contingency plan to cover most eventualities will save you a lot of trouble and inconvenience. A good start is to take some basic but essential provisions with you such as tea bags, chocolate, milk, alcohol, coffee, biscuits, (did I say chocolate and alcohol?) Giving all members going on retreat a central point of contact, i.e. one member's and the proprietors of the venue's mobile number and landline will help should problems occur.

Finding a great venue at a fantastic price and spending a few days with writers who will inspire and motivate you is the best present you can give yourself, your writing and your writing group. Although it might seem a daunting prospect, don't be afraid to try it. Your writing group will be all the better for it and you might find your members fighting over the available places for the next one!

Chapter 4

It's All In The Mind

The Psychology Of Groups

Writing groups are a mishmash of different people living varied lives with a range of beliefs and motives, yet their members come together, meeting after meeting, to share in their one common passion: writing. With such a diverse membership, it's no wonder that things don't always run to plan and sometimes the group dynamics will be off, personalities will clash and the whole atmosphere of the group can change from positive to negative.

Fortunately most writing groups rub along well, but having a little heads up on how groups work from a psychological perspective can help you to prevent issues from getting out of hand or starting in the first place.

Dr Brenda Carter, clinical psychologist, writer and also a member of a writing group, says: "Groups function well because of good leadership and the dynamic interaction between group members that involves everyone. Groups stay stable because of repetition of the interactions and because of repetition of the processes of the group; what happens in group meetings. This means structure to the group but it doesn't have to be rigid. Too much 'set in stone' will stop new ideas and limit new things to do within the group."

So, one way to ensure you have a balanced, effective and good writing group is to ensure that you have some form of structure that binds your members together so they know what to expect but not so restrictive that it stifles their creativity and enjoyment of the group. A little spontaneity goes a long way.

Clinical Psychologist, Dr Lesley Prince, C.Psychol.,AFBPsS, www.lesleyprince.com says, "Just because a collection of people get together and call themselves a writing group doesn't make it so. If some are there purely to improve their writing skills, they will have a very different understanding to those who see it primarily as a social group, with the result that the necessary metaphysical (social) glue that represents or underpins the feeling of groupiness may well be weak or absent. In extreme cases it may result in destructive internal tensions, such as frustration, irritation, anger, etc."

Anyone who has been a member of any group for some time will recognise that variety in members can be a double edged sword. Good for productivity and growth but also a breeding ground for arguments and discord within the group. Change is both necessary and positive in order for that group to function. Groups, as do people, change and fluctuate over time. What your founding members liked and wanted might not be what today's group wants. Groups need to move with the times or run the risk of stagnating and their membership falling.

What Makes Groups Tick?

Dr Carter continues: "All groups have a sense of purpose. They have a common need they wish to be fulfilled and if the group doesn't meet their needs or expectations they won't stay."

So what does Dr Carter think that groups need to allow them to function?

Members – enthusiastic ones!

Someone at the helm to organize, guide and support the group.

A clear set of 'rules', expectations and structure (your constitution).

Fairness – equality, same rules apply to everyone.

All members have a chance to have their say.

Constructive feedback to nurture and motivate.

Flexibility – not all members will want exactly the same thing so you need to adapt.

A calm and supportive atmosphere – no one wants to walk into a group full of underlying seething and jealousy just waiting to erupt!

A fair grievances policy.

"Groups work when there is open communication and all members feel valued, validated and listened to. They also need a chance for members to mingle and get to know each other better. There's nothing worse than walking into a group so obviously separated into different factions and cliques which glare at you with mistrust from their opposing sides, wondering which side you'll take. You can't like everyone but you can agree to disagree and get along for the good of the group."

Dr Prince adds: "As each member is added to the group, the number of relationships increases sharply. Consider the complexity, then, when you consider that at each meeting there will be different numbers of members, with all the relationships that entails. We are 'different people' depending on who is with us; when in the same room as my mum I am a different person to when I am in the same room as my best mate (we have specific prescribed roles); The point is that it is futile to try and control all this complexity, the best one can do is be aware of it, and prepared to meet it when it starts to create negative tensions."

If you are leading the group and you feel the group has lost its connection, it's unity, or you are starting a new group up and don't know how to go about breaking the ice and gelling the group together, what can you do?

Dr Carter suggests:

"Don't force it. Getting to know people in a group can be intimidating and scary for some people. Let nature take its course and natural friendships will form.

Don't force people into sub-groups or partnerships as an ice-breaking activity – it just causes more tension. Let members gravitate to each other naturally.

Try suggesting an informal social event prior to the meetings starting – away from your venue. The pub will do – people may be more relaxed in this neutral environment and knowing a few familiar faces before they come to meetings will make it feel less threatening."

Work It To Your Advantage

We all have different personalities and when they come together in a group situation they will either spark off each other and work well or they will fall apart. Having some background knowledge on the types of people who are group members will help you to organize and run your group better.

Dr Carter says, "Understanding what happens in a group depends on being aware of the roles people take up within it. There are two general types of role that people may take. There are **task-focussed** roles and '**maintenance behaviour roles**' or what I would call **emotional roles.**

Task-focussed roles include:

Initiator: proposes, suggests and defines actions.
Informer: offers facts and opinions.
Clarifier: interprets.
Summariser: restates objectives and concludes a discussion.

Emotional roles include:

Harmonizer: reduces tension and sometimes reconciles differences between group members.
Encourager: is warm and responsive and shows acceptance of others. Someone who is always ready to talk to new members.

Other roles are:

> **Listener**: accepts and follows the ideas put forward by others.
>
> **Time keeper**: keeps everyone to a schedule.
>
> **Tension reliever**: jokes, suggests breaks or exercises. This is important: laughter allows the other group members to express their feelings and lightens the atmosphere.
>
> **Gatekeeper**: facilitates participation, making sure everyone has a space to say something, for instance, to announce a success or suggest a new type of workshop."

Can you recognize any of these traits within your members? Being aware of the different psychological roles that your group members take on can help you to ensure your group integrates and unites as well as provide the positive, inspirational, supportive and motivational atmosphere that group members need.

There will always be a party pooper – that infamous regular Eeyore type character who will not be happy whatever the group does – this is where your tension reliever and encourager come into their own!

Most of the roles within the group are positive and are working together for the good of the group but this is not always the case. Here, Dr Carter warns of more disruptive roles that try and derail proceedings in a variety of dastardly ways!

> "The **Cavalier** plays and jokes inappropriately or for too long, disrupting the group and stopping any more constructive working in the group.
>
> The **Aggressor** attacks ideas, deflates others.
>
> The **Dominator** tries to assert his or her superiority and to manipulate and control. For example, the group can be dominated by a long-winded story teller, who effectively stops others participating, stealing time from more

productive interaction. This role may also be used to block and oppose ideas or group members and can create a very negative atmosphere."

Dr Prince adds: "Fiedler describes three types of groups in terms of their internal behaviours: **interacting groups, co-acting groups** and **counteracting groups**.

> **Interacting groups**: have internal commerce, talking, helping, supporting, etc., etc. Obviously Fiedler thinks this is a 'good' group.
> **Coacting groups:** are like the bus queue; everyone is in the same place doing whatever they do, but what each member does is entirely irrelevant to what each other member does.
> **Counteracting groups:** are internally destructive. Their interactions are conflicted, possibly designed (by some) to weaken the cohesion of the group or prevent it working. Such a group could also be witnessing a power bid as one member (or a group of them) disrupts group dynamics in order to overthrow an existing power structure."

Looking at which group yours most closely resembles can go a long way in helping you to carve the group your members deserve.

Body Language

We are social animals and every part of our body is involved in that intricate dance of communication. But it's not what we say but what we do when we are saying it that often gives away our true feelings and what group leaders need to pay attention to.

How we stand, sit, move our hands, avoid eye contact, stare, lean towards or away from other people, raise our eyebrows, our facial expressions, all tell other people who are attuned to it what we are really feeling. Some body language is quite subtle and can be easy to misinterpret but here are a few examples:

Biting lips or playing with our hair – can be a sign of nervousness.

Clenching fists – can mean anger or frustration.

Fiddling with our hands – can indicate anxiety.

Sitting forward, leaning towards someone – can mean we are interested in them.

Leaning away from someone, arms folded, leg crossed away from them – can be a sign of dislike.

Constantly looking away from someone – can indicate boredom or guilt.

Staring at someone – can be a sign of aggression.

Instead of just concentrating on the verbal communication of your group members, spend some time observing their posture, gestures, facial expressions and movements and this will tell you a lot more about the dynamics and atmosphere of the group. Armed with these tools you can observe your group and 'read' your members to gauge how the meeting is going and learn to communicate more effectively and easily. It is so much less hard work to diffuse a situation before it's in full swing than to wade in mid battle.

Dr Carter says, "With the shared goal of promoting writing and an awareness of the roles people play in groups; with clear leadership and group willingness for harmony, then the experience of the writing group should always be a pleasurable and productive one."

The way forward for your group is balance with the right person as chairperson, a good mix on the committee at the helm and the engendering of a positive and inclusive philosophy for all group members.

Having witnessed a few of the more sticky situations mentioned myself, I understand how difficult being a member of a writing group and being on the committee can be, but the most important aspect for your group has to be communication.

Writers are born communicators in the written form – they may not be so good verbally and socially and a lot can get lost in translation. By paying attention to the body language and psychological roles your members display, you can save yourself and your group a lot of time and hassle.

Chapter 5

Fame At Last

Sharing Your Group's Success

Life is full of celebrations: birthdays, weddings, anniversaries. Big or small they bring people together with a common purpose and your writing group is no exception. With all the rejections and years of toiling without many rewards for your writing, it is important to consider celebrating your writing group. Writing can be a lonely and intense activity and letting your hair down once in a while can be just the tonic disillusioned and rejection weary writers need.

Michael Scullion from Arts Advance writing group is all for celebrating those big anniversaries. "We recently had a 10th anniversary. We hired a room, arranged a buffet, invited old and new members and those who had contributed to our success. We had speeches thanking old and new members and contributors personally, a karaoke of readings by old and new members. We had a free raffle for all attendees and a cake – it was very enjoyable."

Celebrations like Arts Advance enjoyed can be a mixture of formal and informal, engineered to suit the particular needs of your group. All groups are different; what suits Arts Advance might not suit yours so it's important, if you have an anniversary looming, to discuss how members might like to mark the occasion in plenty of time before the big day. It's surprising how much time organisation of these events can take and you may miss out if you don't give yourself sufficient time to plan and get things ready.

Once it has been decided how your group is going to celebrate, it might be more efficient to elect an events team to take on the responsibility of organising the event and then feeding back progress to the rest of the group. This way you will know exactly who in the group to contact should there be any queries and you will know that things are happening behind the scenes to make the event a great success.

You can't hope to have a good celebration without the support of your group members, so it's important to take on the views of all members. You can't please everyone and nor should you try to unless you want to give yourself a headache! But you can ensure that all group members feel part of the celebration from its conception through to the planning, organising and execution of the event.

Giving members roles in this will ensure that all the work is not just left on the shoulders of the few, as can sometimes happen in groups. A few members might be willing to take a share of the load whilst others are only too happy to sit back and let them. Don't be afraid to ask all members for help – they don't have to do anything big or strenuous, but, as the old adage goes – many hands make light work.

The timing of the event is another issue that requires careful consideration. It's generally better to avoid peak holiday times and bank holidays when members may be away and unable to attend. The idea is to allow as many members to attend as possible. Suggest a number of dates as near to your actual anniversary/celebration as possible and opt for the one most members can attend. And, if you decide to go down the same path as Arts Advance, don't forget to invite ex-members (if you are still on speaking terms with them!) and people who you feel have had a positive influence on the group, such as outside speakers who may have done workshops for your group.

You don't have to go for a meal or have a buffet, you can be as adventurous as you like. Some suggestions might be: a sponsored parachute jump, a murder mystery evening, camping, paint balling or a tank driving experience. Wrekin Writers based in Shropshire climbed a local landmark hill, some 1335 ft. tall for their 25th Anniversary.

What you want is a celebration that members aren't likely to forget in a hurry to mark it out as something special. Having ex-members do a karaoke reading session with current members, such as Arts Advance did, is an excellent example of joining the old with the new and helping to make many happy memories for the group they will still be enjoying in years to come.

Pam Fish from NAWG advises, "Make it a special evening so that members can feel satisfied that their success is 'broadcast.' Ask the local paper and radio station to come. This will give great encouragement if the group is prepared to make it something special."

Getting Involved In Local Community And National Events

Once you have got the hang of holding your own celebrations and showcasing your members' work you might want to consider joining forces with other writing groups for some special events.

RMFW did just this, as their program chair Angie Hodapp explains. "I recently booked a speaker whose presentation required projection equipment. I approached another writing organisation that owned a projector and invited them to partner with us on this event. They agreed! So they provided the space and equipment and we brought the food.

"We were also approached by the Mystery Writers of America with a sponsorship offer. They will be offering scholarships to several attendees at our Colorado Gold Conference in exchange for advertising space in our conference booklet."

Linking up with other writing groups at both a local and national level can have benefits for all concerned as Angie has demonstrated, so it is well worth the effort and time to arrange.

Janet Lane, former RMFW Board Member, says "Introducing those who have more knowledge of promotion sharing to other members who have less experience is good. Several writers with common genres or publishers can run an advertisement in a national publication or send out combined library information flyers, pooling funds to get more bang for their bucks."

Forming a committee to handle your media involvement is also a good idea, as Susan Brooks, RMFW conference chair, explains. "We have a publicity committee which writes articles and handles the social media. We collaborate with other writing organisations and sometimes trade a conference registration for advertising, which gets our information to a whole new group of writers who may not have otherwise heard of us."

How To Be A Media Darling

In the world of publicity, image is everything. It's no good having a brilliant writing group if no one knows about you or the work your members do. It's all about promoting your 'brand,' from every angle:

Group name. Professionally run and well organised.
Offer something for everyone.
Have a good social network, including an up to date and eye catching website.
The committee's manner when addressing outside agencies – think polite, accommodating and professional at all times.
Superior quality newsletters and flyers.
Good connections with local and national media: newspapers, radio and TV.

Approaching local and national media will be child's play to writers! So don't forget to keep feeding them details of your upcoming events and any successes members have had. Remember that journalists are writers too and are always on the lookout for interesting stories – use your group's collective creativity to devise a good hook to reel the media in and keep their attention.

What are the important points to remember when wanting to

use the media to publicise your event?

Daniel Burrows, organiser of the Northampton BooQfest says: "It is important to always convey a sense of professionalism and organisation. When you are telling the world about yourself or your organisation, you want people to think that you know what you're doing; that everything is in hand and going as expected – even if this isn't the case behind the scenes!

"I think it is also important to try to maintain the same voice throughout the various channels/mediums that are used. I believe that consistency reassures us that something is OK, so again, helps to convey professionalism and is more likely to succeed as a campaign. The public have a certain level of expectation about public events. If something seems to come across as well-conceived then it is more likely to get public backing. Don't forget that when publicising your event, you are putting your reputation on the line – the reputation of your organisation and of the messenger. Considered communication is the key."

Daniel's committee used the radio as a channel for advertising the festival. "This was free advertising and so it helped us reach a wider audience including those not necessarily social-media savvy (which as a method of advertising accounted for our largest portion)."

So why did Daniel choose social media as the mainstay of his advertising campaign? "Our budget was small and so we purposely sought free publicity through Facebook, Twitter, and posting on various online blogs and 'What's On' guides. Even our website was free. Social media has really changed the face of marketing over the last few years. Through tweeting and re-tweeting, our booQfest team calculated that we'd reached in excess of 2.5 million people in our social media advertising campaign (thanks to re-tweets by celebrities such as Alan Carr). To think that we did this at zero cost makes it one of the most effective means of publicity when viewed on a cost per head basis!"

Does Daniel think that involving the media would be a good thing for writing groups in general?

"It depends on the reason. Why would a writing group need to use the media? To expand the group? If the group is liberal in its outlook, then the media would be a great way to recruit new members if the message was conveyed in a friendly manner that would not deter anyone lacking in confidence. Some writing groups might be closed, or prefer to expand by invitation-only, to ensure a certain level of writing calibre was maintained, in which case media might not be suitable. If the writing group is holding an event they want people to attend, then using the media to publicise this is a must! Media is everywhere!"

Whichever media you choose to advertise your group and events make sure that you get feedback from those who organised it and those who attended it. This is so that you will have a better idea of what worked and what didn't so you can better tailor your media needs.

Chapter 6

Festival Fever

Why Participate?

Once your group is up and running and is into the swing of regular meetings, well run by your wonderful committee, it's time to add a bit of flavour and texture to the menu. There has been an explosion of literary and book festivals in recent years and everywhere you look there is an advert for a literary festival coming to a town near you soon. But is it right for your group and what's in it for you and your group?

A chance for members to prepare some work in time for the deadline of the festival.

An opportunity, not to be missed, for you to showcase your group and its members' talents.

A potential source of income for your group via a writing competition tied in with the festival.

Good advertising for your group to source potential new members or speakers to come to the group.

A chance for the group to meet other writers and writing groups, and network.

A chance to learn new writing skills.

If You Want Something Done Right...

This is all well and good if your area is dripping with festivals to choose from, but what if there isn't a literary or book festival near you? The answer could be to start up your own. Before you run screaming for the hills, it isn't as impossible or scary a task as it might appear.

Daniel Burrows co-organised and ran the first Northampton BooQfest in 2012. He says: "I'd never co-ordinated a project like it before, but found it relatively easy to do so.

"When I started thinking about the content of the festival, I was certain that it would involve authors having slots where they would read from their latest book. I knew that there would be opportunities for the public to ask our visiting authors questions, and to buy signed copies of their books. However, although this was fantastic from an entertainment perspective, I wanted to extend the scope."

When Daniel organised the festival he was daunted but, with limited experience and hard work, he and his team pulled off a stunning festival which was so successful its future is looking very bright. The key to his success was having big ideas but starting off small and simple, gathering a good team to help him, and letting things grow from there.

"I wanted visitors to the festival to leave with something more than just a signed copy of a book. I wanted people to leave feeling inspired. So we used the festival as a showcase for other relevant groups and services in the town. My book group had an introductory spot, as did FAN Northants (the LGBT social events group which partly funded the festival), and Northampton Writers Group. The latter closed the festival with a talk about their group. The idea was to tell the world that they were here and to try to gather some interest and possibly even recruit new members. We also had writing workshops, where anyone could come and explore the art of poetry writing, creative writing or learn about e-books."

Northampton Writers Group was invited to discuss their group at the recent booQfest. Morgen Bailey, chairperson, said, "As well as being an opportunity for local writers to see what one of their groups has to offer, writers from other areas could learn how a writing group runs and even be inspired to start their own."

We can see that when done well, a writing group can be involved as much as they want with a literary or book festival. It's a case of contacting the right people at the right time in the right way. Offering your group's services to volunteer to help out with the organisation and at the actual festival itself is more likely to engage a positive response. Fostering a good working relationship with your community and the agencies housed there is no bad thing.

Susan Brooks, RMFW Conference Chair, says, "The most stressful element for me is getting keynote speakers. Successful writers are busy people. I found that the best solution was to start working on the conference two years in advance and keeping a detailed spreadsheet of what I needed to do when. Organising a conference is a lot of detail to handle and it's impossible to make everyone happy. I just do the best I can.

"If you want to organise an event, especially if you've never done so before, I would recommend that you partner with a mentor who has organised such an event before and who can teach you the details."

My own writing group, Wrekin Writers, has been involved with the Wellington Town Council Literary Festival for some years. They judge their short story competition and also hold a day's workshop on an aspect of writing. It works well.

Pam Fish, chair of NAWG, who hold an annual festival of writing agrees: "Any meeting of like-minded writers is beneficial. The togetherness of a festival atmosphere enables you to talk about your own writing experiences and hear those of others, which can only boost your ego and make you feel like a 'proper' writer. You are no longer that odd person in the family who writes, but part of a writing community, amongst writers just like yourself."

Pam Nowak, RMFW, says, "During my tenure as conference chair, I discovered several things very quickly:

1. Organisation was essential, at every single level in every single task.

2. Delegate, delegate, DELEGATE!

3. Numbers 1 and 2 only work if you have the right volunteers. And if you do, you can accomplish just about anything."

Setting Up

Daniel suggests this: "In terms of setting up a festival, I didn't do it alone. I wasn't responsible for fund raising, which is probably the hardest part! We started with a small idea – a one-off literary event rather than a 'festival'. But it just seemed to take on a life of its own and grow! We were aware of something very exciting happening and were therefore very lucky to meet generous people and organisations along the journey who also sensed this and were able to support us, to make it happen.

"Festivals need funding, a venue (or venues) and content. If the venture is commercial, then it probably also needs ticket sales! Ours was not. It was funded by charitable donations and we wanted to provide a service, not make profit. All events at our festival were free of charge.

"Organising the literary festival was a thoroughly rewarding experience and I personally found it very inspiring. After having the unique opportunity to speak with respected and celebrated published authors on a one-to-one basis, I have been inspired to start writing myself and have formed a small writing group at my place of work. I hope other visitors of the festival were inspired too. We received a lot of very positive feedback from the festival, which was great considering it was our first one."

Things To Consider

Date & time
Venue
Agenda of events

Numbers of visitors expected

Speakers

Refreshments

Fees: This splits in to outgoings and income – venue hire, speaker fees, first aid, insurance, entrance fees etc.

Public Liability Insurance : your chosen venue should have this if they hold events regularly, so do ask about this before you book. You don't want a member of the public attending the festival to injure themselves, leaving you to pay compensation out of the group's funds! The Health and Safety Executive has excellent advice on running events safely on www.hse.gov.uk/event-safety/index.htm

Risk Assessments: see online sites such as the Health and Safety Executive on www.hse.gov.uk/risk/fivesteps.htm for advice on ensuring your chosen venue is safe. Talk to the venue managers too as they should have done risk assessments, especially if they regularly hold functions there.

First Aid: most venues will have a first aid box but are there qualified first aiders in your group who might be willing to help out on the day? Try St. John's Ambulance on www.sja.org.uk or the Red Cross on www.redcross.org.uk, both of whom run first aid courses and may provide first aiders for events. If you have a member who is a qualified first aider and who is willing to be the designated first aider for your event, check out the venue's insurance first to make sure they are covered.

Publicity: advertising the event.

Attracting Visitors

If you are concerned that no one will turn up, don't forget that you always have your writing group to attend! Expect smaller numbers for your first festival and if you get more, well that's a bonus! Remember that advertising is your friend here, as are the local media. Get on the local TV, radio stations and newspapers, free community newsletters and other such publications, put posters up in local shops, library, GP surgery, any public place that will take them.

National UK magazines for writers such as Writing Magazine (www.writers-online.co.uk), Writers' Forum (www.writers-forum.com) and The New Writer (www.thenewwriter.com) and for the USA The Writer (www.writermag.com) or Writers' Digest (www.writersdigest,com/magazines) all carry space for advertising festivals – an article on your festival might go down well too, especially the ins and out of organising it.

Local colleges and universities that carry writing courses would be good to approach too – they could inform students about the event and also advertise it on their website.

Local bookshops, both chain and independent, might help too and approaching related businesses to sponsor the event in turn for some publicity could be a nice little earner and help you to fund the event.

Post Mortem

Don't forget to canvass attendees to see what they liked and disliked about the festival. Their views are vitally important to help you assess the overall success of the event and to iron out any creases for future events. Sit down with your festival committee and discuss, honestly and openly, what worked well and what could be improved. How did the local council, press and venue managers feel the event went? If you had any sponsors, what were their feelings?

Pay attention and resist the urge to be defensive about your 'baby.' Listen and learn and prepare for an even bigger and better festival the following year. Give your potential festival attendees what they want and you'll have them coming back for more year after year.

Chapter Seven

When Things Go Wrong

When a group of people are together, it's inevitable that there will be personality clashes and some disagreement. Creative people can be sensitive and their moods can be a little extreme, especially when dealing with their own precious work, so it's not surprising that tempers might flare. How can writing groups reduce the risk of such issues in their own group?

Bad Things Happen To Good Writing Groups

Although preparation and planning are key to the survival and success of any writing group, even the best laid plans can unravel and leave you and your writing group in trouble. The important thing to remember is that some issues that might crop up are beyond your control and that you can't predict everything that might go wrong.

Judith Taylor from The Writers' Block says: "Be prepared to talk things through and accept that there will be disagreements. These should be regarded as resulting from differing points of view, not 'right' and 'wrong'. Any criticism should be constructive, and the critic should be able to explain exactly what they think should be improved, and why."

When issues do arise, e.g. one member monopolising the meetings, disagreements between members, members being rude to or dismissive of other members' work, etc., how can writing groups deal with it?

Susan MacKay Smith, former RMFW President, advises, "Personality clashes will happen in any group of people. RMFW has had its share. We've also been lucky that our member-elected boards have had the intelligence and dedication to handle the problems *within* the board (not gossiping to the general membership) and as grown-ups. In other words, while we have dealt with problems, even to dismissing members, the dirty laundry never airs."

One of the major bones of contention that can arise within writers' groups is strong personalities monopolising the meetings, leaving no opportunity for less vocal members to have their say. Members such as this usually either have no idea they are taking over the meeting or they are only too well aware and love the sound of their own voice too much to care about anyone else's feelings and needs.

Pam Fish from NAWG has this suggestion to help: "To prevent this there must be a fair way of hearing everyone's work. Also unless the person taking the meeting is aware of this, less able writers may be crushed. Lots of emotions may be triggered – jealousy, envy, to name a couple. Everyone must be kind and supportive to each other. And, on the negative side, there shouldn't be any gossip about members, even joke-like comments can be quite hurtful.

"There should be a mild kind of probation for new members and if they really don't 'click' with most people then they should at first be reminded that 'we don't do things like that' or, as a last resort to maintain the harmony of the existing group, they should be asked to leave. Only have members who are friends or friends of friends and use the above for unknown people (the probation bit). A good harmonious and friendly group will put off those who are selfishly trying to join solely for their own writing.

"A strong core of writers who are united in their ideals can be very off-putting to troublemakers. So, stick to your principles and the chances are that those who were trying to monopolise, be rude, dismissive, etc., will get bored with trying if they get nowhere and will leave of their own accord. If all else fails, a discreet word in their ear should do the trick."

Toni Neville from Weymouth & Portland U3A writing group says: "From hearsay, I know of one group that folded because the members objected to a very 'bossyboots' know-it-all who tried to impose his views and will on the others, and was scathing in his criticism."

Other groups have reported personality clashes leading to arguments amongst group members and an uncomfortable atmosphere, resulting in offending members being asked to mend their ways or leave. Not a good place for a writing group to be.

Janet Lane, RMFW Board Member, recalls a sticky situation she had to deal with. "I had to remove a writer from our group because she couldn't separate her religious views from fiction and kept trying to convince another member that her history was faulty and she should re-write certain segments of her novel to suit this writer's personal beliefs. This situation was touchy and difficult, but her dismissal was necessary to remove the toxic element from the group."

Other issues that might arise:

Your meeting place becomes unavailable and you have to find a new venue.

A sudden or gradual drop in members and difficulty in recruiting new members.

Cash flow problems.

Difficulties in getting enough members to volunteer to take a role on the committee.

Disagreements between members on how the group should be run.

The Writers' Group Toolbox

At some point all writing groups will encounter problems and if you can't prevent them you can choose to deal with them effectively by using the right tools in your Writing Group Tool Box.

Your committee: this is probably the most versatile and useful tool in your tool box. Having a good, supportive and proactive team working with you to run the group is essential and, proving the adage that two heads are better than one and a problem shared is a problem halved, they will help you get out of all sorts of sticky situations.

A good sense of humour: lighten up and take the small stuff with a pinch of salt. Learn to know which battles to fight and which to let go. Introducing some light heartedness can help to diffuse potentially difficult situations. However, be warned, too much light heartedness could also go the other way with some members feeling ridiculed.

Perspective: taking a step back and breathing will give you time to assess whether the problem is really that bad and explore your options in solving it.

A repertoire of emergency activities: if a speaker lets you down at the last minute, make sure you have something to pull out of the bag to keep members entertained.

Contacts: build up a good contacts list of people with a range of knowledge, and expertise list so you can call on the 'experts' should a problem you are having difficulties with arise.

Pamela Nowak, RMFW, suggests this: "I encountered personality issues as conference chair from finicky agents to headstrong presenters to needy volunteers to intoxicated speakers to attendees with special needs we were unaware of until there was a problem.

"Anyone can be difficult – more so if they've had a bad day, are confused or don't know the reasoning behind the action. Always, always be professional. Try to lessen problems and head them off before they happen. Sometimes just listening, answering questions, or offering explanations can diffuse problems.

"Be ethical and remember that you represent the group. Use written procedures if you have them. Be aware that how you handle situations can set precedents for the future. If you always try to be fair and professional and avoid being reactive, most problems can be solved."

Don't forget to use what you learned in chapter four about what makes groups tick. Applying a bit of your new-found psychological knowledge will go a long way to getting you out of and keeping you out of trouble. But remember, at the heart of how you deal with issues that arise within your writing group should be the group's ethos – its reason for being and its constitution. Remember why you started the group in the first place and, when the going gets rough, take comfort in the fact that you are doing your best to help fellow writers on their way. Stick to your group's principles and you won't go far wrong.

In this chapter we can see why a group's constitution and committee is a good idea. If members' attention is drawn to the constitution and expectations of group members are pointed out, disruption should be kept to a minimum. A good committee will also back you up should things go wrong through no fault of your own. There is a strength and safety in numbers. Decisions in a writing group should be made by the committee for each member's own interests and in the spirit of fairness.

Common Problems And How To Deal With Them

Dr Lesley Prince has these suggestions to help you with the most common issues that might adversely affect writing groups.

One member trying to monopolise the meetings and not giving other members a chance to get a word in edgeways.

"They may regard themselves as the group 'leader' in some sense, and this may be based on their estimation of their own skill and experience. On the other hand it may be that they are unaware of other people and their needs. This is not necessarily selfishness, just a lack of awareness. It might be an out and out power play, perhaps linked to low self esteem (as power plays so often are). Of course they may simply be narcissistic and therefore discount other people's concerns as unworthy of anyone's attention. Another explanation is that they may be so insecure that they are terrified of being shown up for the charlatan that they feel themselves to be, and what better way of preventing that than by monopolising the space and preventing the dangerous truth from being revealed.

"If I were in the group, I would expect someone to tell them quite sharply to shut up. It suggests the need of a proper chair convening the meeting, or at least an acknowledged facilitator who is given the authority to do so by agreement of the group."

Long standing dislikes that have festered between certain members over the years that sometimes spill over and cause problems.

"If the group is to survive, this sort of thing cannot be allowed because it will render the group incapable of functioning on occasions. It may create cliques around the protagonists, or render the rest of the membership mute for fear of causing a row. Again a proper chair or facilitator seems necessary. Clearly a rivalry brought from the outside has nothing to do with the group's activities, and the protagonists, therefore, should be made aware that their row belongs outside.

When faced with these kinds of situations groups that try to resolve the situation, generally respond by laddering their interventions:

Step 1:**Persuasion** by reasoned argument.
Step 2: **Seduction** by promising some desirable reward.
Step 3: **Threat** of some undesirable sanction.
Step 4: **Expulsion** from the group.

Finding a way of compromise acceptable to the warring factions is often recommended, and where this is not possible separation is the preferred strategy."

New members joining the group, claiming to be writers, when they are, in fact, just wanting to use the group as a platform to air their grievances or discuss their health problems, etc.

"They are in the wrong group and should be told so. Again, clear structure helps. If they need counselling, it should be done away from the group, or the group will not survive."

Disagreements within the group about how the group should be run.

"This is a common one, and very tricky. I would expect this to occur most often in new groups or groups that have just recruited some rather confident newbies. It's part of the process known as orientation, when the group tries to get itself organised for action. Since it is a fundamental question about the group's operation, it really is something that each group MUST resolve sooner or later. All groups need some minimal amount of structure in order to be able to operate at all. From my experience, groups that are too open-ended and unstructured end up doing nothing at all. But structure need not be authoritarian and inflexible, indeed I would suggest it SHOULD NOT be authoritarian and inflexible.

"There are many ways of tackling this issue. For example appointing a chair or facilitator whose job it is to see that the group sessions swing along at a pace suitable for the group's activities, making sure nobody monopolises the sessions, keeping people roughly on track, giving room to people whose sensibilities may have been disturbed, unruffling feathers, and so on.

Chair or facilitator roles need not be fixed either, but can be rotated amongst the group's members from meeting to meeting, giving everyone a chance to run a session the way they would prefer. Over time the group as a whole will learn what suits its own temperament best."

Members giving other members brutal critiques on their work within the group setting – not being constructive.

"This strikes me as a power play, pure and simple. Such behaviour will eventually discourage people from attending, from sharing their work, or even from writing at all. It's purely destructive and can only result in an elitist closed group, or no group at all."

Chapter Eight

Going International

Once you have organised a couple of events for your writing group and your local area you might want to consider looking further afield to build networks and new links. A good writing group will expand and change with its growing members and their developing needs. Writing groups cannot afford to stand still and stagnate.

A festival in your locality can bring many benefits to your group: income, new members, a higher public profile to name but a few, but widening your network can increase your group's opportunities. There are hundreds of excellent writing groups that you can contact, especially other members of NAWG but there are advantages to casting your net overseas too.

Buddy Building

Just as towns are sometimes twinned with other towns abroad, why not think about starting your own writing group 'twinning' project? Think foreign exchange students from when you were at school. The details of thousands of writing groups across the globe are just a click away and buddying up with a few can increase your potential network of expertise at the click of a button. Think about it. It can be especially helpful if:

> You want to set your short story, novel, etc., in a certain part of the world you've not been to. You can just contact a writing group in that area and ask for their input. You want advice on legal, police, government procedures which are different on your own home turf.
> You wish to add a bit of realism and colour to your writing by asking someone who lives in the place you are writing

about for details such as the smells, temperature, sights and sounds they encounter there – something you can't fully experience over the internet.

Details of cuisine, money, housing, clothes, customs, traditions, daily life, etc., can be gained from people who live there and know it.

You could have links on your website to various writing groups abroad and start an international forum where members of your group and those abroad can interact and make friends and contacts.

You want to make new friends and consider the possibility of organising a future exchange visit for a few members.

Susan Brooks, RMFW Conference Chair, says, "I am all for collaboration and leveraging other groups. We have worked with other organisations locally and have had keynote speakers from abroad, but we haven't yet linked with another writing group abroad. I think it would be very interesting if we could provide some kind of writing retreat exchange program with other writing groups. Some of them could come and write in Colorado, USA, and some of us could go to their home and write there. The change of scenery could be amazingly inspiring."

Moving/Holidays Abroad

If you are already a member of a writing group or have set up your own and then you move abroad, or are taking an extended holiday overseas but you don't want to lose the strong, invaluable links you've worked hard to gain, what can you do?

Paul Connell moved to Spain in 2007 and spent time exploring his options before setting up All Angles writing group four years ago (webfacil.tinet.org/allangles)." I looked around for outlets for English language writing – there were none. I had been a member of a very successful and helpful group in Perth, Scotland, and thought I might try to replicate that. I expected to attract immigrants or expats like me, but what I found was a group of local people writing in Catalan and English."

Paul took his time in creating the right writing group for him but it wasn't easy. If you rush it without giving proper consideration to planning (remember the three P's in chapter 1: Preparation, Persistence and Production?), you might find your efforts come to nothing. Although there will be some similarities in how writing groups work abroad, there will also be differences that might be unique to that country or area which you will need to research before setting up your own group or finding a good existing group.

Paul's advice to other writers moving abroad and wanting to find a writing group is, "Don't go in with any preconceptions – exploit all and any networks there are available locally but be prepared to create your own if necessary. Use all group members to identify activities, resources and ideas – even if you start something, you don't own it. Let it develop as it wants to develop."

Bondi Writers http://(www.bondiwritersgroup.org.au), based in Australia, was formed seven years ago and is run in a similar way to groups in the UK. Anne Skyvington, the group's Communications Officer, says, "We hold an Annual General Meeting to elect our management committee: president, secretary, treasurer, communications officer and membership secretary. The president is the spokesperson for the group. He convenes monthly meetings, organises speakers, heads committee meetings and liaises with our umbrella organisation, the NSW Fellowship of Australian Writers."

But what are the main difficulties that an Australian writing group faces that resonate with those in other countries? Anne explains, "One of the hardest things is to have sustained input from members in order to keep the group going. As all positions are voluntary and members are normally very willing to assist with special events, but sometimes the roles of president and treasurer are not easy to fill and it's often a steep learning curve for new post holders."

Paul, founder of All Angles, agrees that local and national associations that assist writing groups make the whole experience easier: "Once we got going we established contact with groups in Barcelona and Girona – through the offices of Catalonia Today magazine, an English language publication in Barcelona, whose representative has been crucial in the whole thing."

Paul was lucky in that he found the help and advice he needed fairly quickly and, as a result of that continued support, All Angles is thriving but it might not have been the case without the contacts he found.

Susan Siddeley formed Santiago Writers, based in Chile. The group is also thriving. One of their members attended the recent NAWG Writing Festival, the group having won the anthology competition. She says: "Writing Groups are wonderful, precious things. I know we are all grateful, in awe even, of what ours has achieved!

"We write in English but all our members are bi-lingual or fluent in Spanish. Our strength lies in our need to learn and practice the craft of writing in our first language. When we started meeting in the late 1990s, it was expensive and difficult getting materials. This is not true these days with the internet, but a hands-on group, meeting weekly, cannot be beat!"

Funding in the UK for writing groups can be an issue but what is the situation in other countries? Anne from Bondi Writers says: "We get funding from our local Council. This enables us to continue to hold our competitions, events and workshops. The Council also enables us to use the Library where we hold our meetings and public events without charge."

What about in Spain? Paul explains: "Existing organisations, e.g. the British Council, could perhaps be more sensitive to unofficial grassroots activity outside the usual cultural institutions, though I know they are as strapped for cash as any public body nowadays so I'm not criticising them."

So how can you go about it?

Go online. Are there local writing groups in the area you are moving to/holidaying? Introduce yourself.

Shop around. If you can't find a suitable group, consider setting one up yourself.

Try a 'twinning' approach by connecting your local writing group in the UK to one abroad – exchange visits could be fun!

Take note of local laws and procedures for forming and running writing groups abroad. They may be different to those in your locality.

Ask for advice from other writing groups in the same country.

Chapter Nine

Online Options

Don't Be Shy!

The Internet – there's no escaping it these days. It can be both a blessing and a curse and writing groups should think carefully before setting up an online presence. The first question writing groups need to ask themselves is do they need an online profile?

Louise Gibney, member of Towcester Writing Group, suggests that they do: "Websites are a great way to reach people and to be seen online. In this day and age, people expect to find a website when they search online for a group, service or business. In conjunction with a Facebook page and some traditional printed publicity of course, a group website can really boost your profile locally and nationally."

Which One?

So what are the options open to writing groups if they want to get an online profile?

Morgen Bailey runs and belongs to four different writing groups. She says, "I have blogs on WordPress and Blogspot. Whilst they can be much simpler than mine, they can look very professional in a short amount of time. I'd also recommend joining the NAWG (National Association of Writing Groups) as you would then get listed on their http://www.nawg.co.uk/ writing-groups page."

Louise suggests social networking sites might be a good alternative to begin with. "A Facebook page is quick and easy to set up and can be a powerful tool in spreading the word about your group. In the first 6 months of Towcester's Facebook page being launched, we had over 40 members when monthly turn-out averages about 18 writers."

Morgen says, "There are other ways to be active online. If any of the group's members are active on social networks such as Twitter and Facebook then they can draw other writers (and potential new members) to the group's site. Having their writing on sites such as authonomy.com (Harper Collins' critique site) and youwriteon.com is another way to glean feedback, although you have to give as much as you get in most cases by critiquing other writers' work, often at random, but again this is a great, if not time-consuming, networking opportunity."

So what other options are there? Louise suggests, "There are many good free web hosting tools you can register with (e.g. Weebly, where my writers' group is hosted – www.towcester-writers.weebly.com) as long as you don't mind having them advertise their services on your web address. You obviously pay to have a website developed and hosted in a 'clean' URL address link, but this isn't always necessary. Check within your group – someone may have the appropriate skills to lend a hand."

Pam Nowak, RMFW, suggests, "My advice is to do research. Have members knowledgeable about website software be a part of designing any requests for proposals, vetting of proposals or design itself."

Staying On The Right Side Of The Line

But are there any pitfalls? Vicki Law, RMFW Education Chair and PR Chair, has this word of warning: "We have experienced growing pains. Volunteers don't always agree with the Board on what is acceptable to post online and what isn't. How does a board of volunteers reprimand a single volunteer who has freely given their time and is as enthusiastic about the organization as any one serving on the board? However, as a board, we decided that RMFW's professional image is of utmost importance.

"In one situation we lost our blog over disagreements between the board and the volunteer who started the blog. We had no control over content and could do nothing to maintain ownership, though the site held itself as the 'official' Rocky Mountain Fiction Blog."

What are the benefits of a writing group getting a profile online? Morgen Bailey says, "Apart from letting the wider public know that you exist, you can post your work on your site and advertise events. With so much going on online these days, it's almost a necessity. It's also an opportunity for your members to sell their books – whether directly and/or putting links to Amazon, Smashwords, Lulu, CreateSpace etc."

"Posting items on a blog also attracts others to comment and interact with your members. It's reaching an audience that they wouldn't have had otherwise and you never know who is going to find you."

It sounds easy when you know how but what difficulties might a writing group face when trying to set up an online profile?

Morgen says, "Getting a free blog up and running is easy but you do need a little I.T. knowledge. For example, http://wordpress.com is the starting point for WordPress. Just sign up (which is free) and follow the instructions for creating a new blog."

Getting Started

Start with a simple website and let it grow from there.

The first piece of information you need on your website is when and where the group meets – obviously!

Link your website and blog to your Facebook, Twitter, LinkedIn, Yahoo and Tumblr accounts automatically so every time you post a blog it can automatically appear on any or all of those pages, saving a huge amount of time... which can be better spent writing.

Keep the content up to date. Visitors want to know the page is current and well-maintained.

Always ask permission of the subjects before posting photos of people.

Ensure someone keeps an eye on the website or Facebook page to respond to queries.

Make sure you use words people may Google to find you in the title of the page and the first few lines published on the homepage.

Acknowledging local writing events and other groups is a nice touch.

The trick is for people to know that it exists and most people search via sites such as Google and Yahoo, so you would need to appear fairly high up in the results. Posting something new each week (as a minimum) will also help have more listings in the results, especially if you use keywords that people would look for.

Above tips from Morgen Bailey, Louise Gibney and Mark Stevens.

Getting an online profile for your writing group is a good way to publicise yourselves and get more members as well as allowing you to keep your members and potential members up to date. A few simple steps and clicks will soon set you up.

Chapter Ten

Competition Challenge

To Run One Or Not To Run One?

Don't run before you can walk is good advice in any situation, not least when you are first starting up a writing group. Taking a slow but steady approach will benefit you and your group in the long run. So starting up a writing competition is best left until your group is strong in both constitution, committee and members.

Organising and running a writing group competition is not an easy task and involves a lot of hard work which you, as group founder, will have to shoulder unless you have a keen, knowledgeable and efficient team behind you. You might want to consider, as in all things writing group related, to think big but start small.

Wrekin Writers undertake a mini chairman's challenge each month where the chairman sets a theme with a 100 word limit and members are invited to make their entry anonymously. The entries are judged and the winner receives a small monetary reward and a selection of entries are published in their anthology each year.

This is an excellent place to start as it involves minimal organisation. You could then move on to having a group-wide short story competition or poetry competition with a bigger word count and bigger prize. Once you've got your head around that you can begin to think about holding a national or even international writing competition. But you're going to have to take a lot into consideration before you take that leap.

Getting Started

Sally Quilford, quillersplace.wordpress.com, writer, author and columnist, runs the Competition Calendar and column in

Writers' Forum. Having both entered and judged writing competitions for some years, she has seen what is involved from both sides. So what does she think are the most important things to remember when setting up your own writing competition?

"It's a good idea to work out exactly what you expect from the comp and how you all want it to be run.

Decide who is doing what: judge, reader, organiser. There is a lot of work involved in running a competition so don't put it on one person's shoulders. Have a back-up plan, in case of illness or some other crisis.

I would suggest keeping writing group comps and open comps separate. By all means have small internal comps to reward your members for their hard work, but when it comes to open comps it's better to keep it to outsiders only. That way you don't risk any questions about members winning an open comp.

Have realistic expectations about what your group hopes to achieve by running a competition. It may take several years for a writing group comp to become established, and so for a while you may not make anything from it.

Think about why you want to run a writing comp. If it is to make money for the group, that's fine. There's nothing wrong with that. But as I've said before, be prepared for that not happening straight away. Look at things in the long term, and be willing to spend time building up a good reputation.

Be sure that your group, as a whole, can take on this task. Can you trust everyone involved in the competition process to do their job? It's important that everyone has a realistic view of what they're taking on.

Sometimes what seems to be a simple thing can become very complicated. Running a writing comp involves administration, which includes keeping records, keeping the entries safe, data protection (you have a duty to protect the personal details of all who enter), dealing with queries, LOTs of reading, and then dealing with the aftermath. This may include disgruntled losers who will complain no matter how well the comp was run.

All these things need to be decided before you even begin to promote your competition."

Susan Mackay Smith, former RMFW Contest Chair, says, "We regard our contest as a teaching tool for writers wanting to advance their craft. What seems to be astonishingly difficult for a large number of entries each year is following the contest rules for format. Our formatting rules track those the publishing industry has demanded for years. Our contest wants to teach writers to pay attention to details, because following the rules (or not) may still be the difference between a rejection or a contract."

There's a lot to think about isn't there! But don't be put off by it all. There are lots of writing groups out there that do their own writing competitions as proof that it can and is being done very successfully. Focus on how a writing competition can enhance your group with an eye on what might go wrong.

Why Run Your Own Competition?

So what can a writing competition do for your group?

Get your group's name known.

Allow group members to develop their organising and judging skills.

Provide the group with most welcome and much needed funds.

Allow members to enter the competition, if allowed, and give them the confidence to enter others.

Improve members' reading skills which will in turn improve their own stories.

Janie Mason from RWA says, "We've found that judging contests is a great way for writers to learn. Oftentimes, it makes you aware of things to avoid, or attempt, in your own writing."

Running Like Clockwork

The above are the main advantages of running your own writing competition but Sally has a word of warning.

"On the con side, I have known writers' groups competitions that are very incestuous. This can happen when there's a leader (or leaders) with very specific ideas about what 'real' writing is. Then when the comp is run, even if it is open to the public, it's almost impossible for anyone outside the group to win. The main problem with that is that those outside the group then feel they've only been used to raise funds so that the organisers' friends can cash in. I've seen this happen, and it leads to bitterness all around.

"Another con is that you may not raise the funds you hoped to raise. Keep your expectations realistic. There is a chance you won't make up the prize fund, so it's wise to have a back-up plan there too. What will you do if not enough people enter? Will you refund entry fees? Or will the prizes come out of the group's funds?"

Terry Wright, former RMFW Contest Chair, says, "The downside of running a contest such as our Colorado Gold Writing Contest is the tremendous amount of work required to pull off a successful contest."

But it's still worth your group running its own writing competition, as Susan Mackay Smith attests: "The contest benefits contestants who don't final. The biggest benefit is then being given a genuinely objective assessment of their work. Contests can also be valuable to writers who lack other writerly contact, and feedback can show them where their strengths lie and what areas they need to focus on.

"RMFW itself benefits greatly from the contest. Since we charge for submissions, with extra for an in-depth written critique, the contest is a money maker. Though we give cash prizes to the finalists, we still make money, which helps to fund our other educational programs throughout the year. The contest also attracts new members as they learn about us through the contest, especially as we try hard to make the contest a positive experience."

Rules Are Rules

Once you've done all the hard work involved in thinking about your competition – who's going to run it and how, what the prizes will be, who will judge it and how, and any contingency plans you need – running your competition shouldn't be a nightmare as long as you follow your own plans and rules to the letter. Don't give disgruntled writers who didn't make the short list any excuse to pick you up on any inconsistencies in your organisational or judging process.

Sally has this advice to keep you on the right track:

"Rules need to be simple, easily accessible and they have to make sense.

The most important rules should cover word or line length, the fee and how to pay it, the prizes, where to send entries, and most prominently, the closing date.

Whilst the rules can cover other elements like preferred font and size and whether a story can be typewritten or handwritten, leave out the trivial stuff about staples vs. paper clips etc.

Be prepared to pay out the prizes as soon as possible when the comp has closed. It's bad karma for writing comps to withhold prize monies from winners.

Make sure there are proper prizes, and not just a promise to people to be published in an anthology which they must buy in order to see."

Pamela Nowak from RMFW found good organisation was key for their writing competition. "Another key to a good contest is the score sheet. As a former entrant to writing contests, I loved organisations that had a well-rounded, detailed score sheet that assured judges were scoring based on objective factors rather than whether or not they liked the entry. Objectivity is a must."

Having judged a number of the Doris Gooderson Short Story Competitions run by my writing group Wrekin Writers and the Wellington Town Council Short Story Competition, I can advise that having the statement along the lines of, "If it doesn't say you can do it, then you can't!" at the end of your list of competition rules will save you a lot of headaches. As will having contact details of your competition secretary or administrator so potential entrants can check if they have a query.

Remember that your set of rules needs to be fair but forthright and that if you disqualify stories for not following the rules, you must be able to prove how the offending stories disregarded your rules.

Mistakes DO happen. I once mislaid the winning entrant's story! Not my finest moment but I was forgiven, a lesson was learned and another copy was gained and all was well. So don't get too anxious about it all and enjoy the process and think of your first winning entrant's beaming smile as their story is showcased on your website and they receive that cheque!

Writers who enter your competition will have spent a great deal of time and effort producing their piece of work. Remember, they have chosen your competition out of the hundreds of others out there, so the least they expect is for you to run your competition properly, which you can now do!

I hope from reading this book that you can see that although joining a writing group or starting your own is challenging and hard work, it's also motivating and rewarding. The advice in this book, from experienced writing groups from around the world, will set you well on your way to discovering the best writing group for you. Watch your writing group's and your writing career fly when you do.

Julie Phillips

Chapter Eleven

A Change Is As Good As A Rest

20 workshop/activity ideas for your writing group

The following activities are designed to help you keep your writing group motivated, inspired and, most importantly, to write and to come back for more by encouraging you to introduce some variety to your meetings and workshops.

While you can't hope to please everyone you should find something for even the most difficult to please member in the following suggestions.

Find Your Inner Child: Play Doh, Lego, feely boxes with cold tinned spaghetti or baked beans hiding inside, or jelly, the childish the better as you play your way to inspiration.

Feely Boxes: Blindfold your members and ask them to place their hands into the boxes in front of them. The point is for them to describe what they can feel with their hands and hazard a guess as to the contents of the boxes. By encouraging them to use just one of their senses, touch, will help readers to become more aware of the sense of touch and its importance in their writing.

You can also do it with smells, sounds and taste too by obscuring the other senses in some way so they have to focus on just one sense at a time. Their resulting writing will be all the more colourful for it.

Children are incredibly creative and are encouraged to be so. They paint, draw, stick and glue to their heart's content – something we sadly begin to lose as we get older. But by encouraging your members to find their inner child again you can rejuvenate your members' flagging enthusiasm and boost their creativity.

I heartily encourage all writers to spend time with children if they can – they are not only a constant source of hilarity but they will also inspire your writing and give you a spring in your step again. Also, indulging in activities which children enjoy and revisiting your own childhood play time activities can put a spring back in your step. Go on – get on that space hopper. You know you want to!

Playtime: Get the Lego, Play Doh, Meccano, boxes, anything you can lay your hands on that will encourage your members to build something. By playing in this way, members will be using their creativity in a different form which will boost their own creative writing.

Ask members to describe the planning and building process. Did they have an idea in their head of what they were going to build or was it completely spontaneous and they just went where the Lego took them? This activity is a great practical way to show members the differences between planning their writing and not.

Genre Gallop: have each member think of an idea for a short story, poem or novel then ask them to write a short blurb for that idea in a romantic style. Then alter it to a horror style, then a fantasy style, then a crime style, etc. The more genres the better.

The idea here is to help dispel the myth that you pick a genre and stick with it. Often, when writing, writers can't pin point what is wrong with a piece that isn't working for them and it could be that their chosen genre is wrong. By encouraging your members to try out different styles and genres you are opening up a whole new set of opportunities to them – opportunities they might never have considered before.

Write Me A Line: each group member writes a line, folds it up and passes it to another member who writes another line and then to another member who writes the third line. This is your beginning line, mid-point line and ending to a story – pass each three lines on to a different member and they fill in the gaps.

This activity will get your members used to writing within a pre-determined framework where they already have the beginning line, middle line and end point of a story. This really works the creative muscles and the end results can be stunning – you may have the framework for a cracking short story or be able to work elements of it into a novel.

This also works well with words. Have each member pick out three words from a hat. The words can be names, places, moods, objects, personality traits, situations, problems, etc., and have them come up with a story line for a play, short story, novel, poem or even an article idea.

Poetry of Passion: Have a sheet of a selection of themes, objects, emotions, places and poetry forms and cut them up. Put them in separate piles and ask each member to pick one from each pile, e.g., theme: autumn, object: umbrella, emotion: hatred, place: a church, poetry form: sonnet. Each member writes a poem or notes for a poem around this.

This activity is ideal for members to learn to write poetry through practise as having definitions and examples of the various forms of poems pinned up around the room you meet in and with a set of words to base it on will help even the most poem phobic member to have a go.

Pick a Poem: Have some unusual objects secreted around the room and ask members to find an object that piques their interest and write down as many words and phrases they can in 60 seconds about that object.

This is good for developing an eye and ear for what works well within poetry and focuses the mind to the task in hand. It also shows members that inspiration can come from the most mundane and usual objects and observations as well as the more exotic.

Word Wrangler: word association game. The object is for one member to shout out the first word that comes into their head followed by the next member and so on. Put a time limit of 60 seconds for each round around the room. The pressure is on, often with hilarious consequences! Make sure someone records the words for inspiration (and a laugh) later!

This activity is not only good for making members laugh and loosen up – it makes a brilliant ice breaker – it's also good for creating associations and the thread of a poem or short story in the brain. This association might not be obvious at first, but the seeds will have been sown and the idea will grow, to be reaped at a later date.

Collage Me A Story: place pictures of everything and anything around the room for each member to collect and stick on an A3 sheet of paper to form a story, poem or idea for a novel.

Often, seeing a picture of a place, person, object, etc., can trigger a story idea which can be worked on.

Pitch It To Me: one for budding article writers. Have some members as magazine editors and the rest as budding article writers – give members a selection of up to date magazines and ask them to look through them and come up with article ideas for the magazine they will pitch to the editors.

This, if your editors are seasoned, published article writers, can help members to hone their pitching skills and learn what works, makes their pitch sparkle and places it above those of other writers.

Hit Me With Your Rhythm Stick: it's all about the beat. Bring in anything that makes a sound – make your own shakers, drums, anything that produces sound and try out different rhythms to set and read your writing out to.

The purpose of this activity is to help you hear and appreciate the different rhythms and paces within your own and others' writing. It allows you to hear if that sentence or phrase sounds right and how it could be improved.

Word Detectives: It's time to make like Sherlock Holmes with your magnifying glass in hand and deer stalker hat and get to the bones of words and their origins and meanings. Ask each member to pick an unusual or rarely used word and bring it to the group along with dictionaries, thesaurus, laptops, whatever you have. Have a guess at trying to think of the meaning of the word and put it into a sentence before you find out the true meaning – warning: this activity can cause an excess of hilarity!

Photograph Fanatics: Go outside in the locality where your group meets and ask members to bring their digital cameras and get snapping – the more the obscure and abstract the better. Load them onto some laptops and see the inspiration spark.

Article Antics: I can't write about that! Oh yes you can! Find some outlandish themes, the more obscure the better – the challenge is for members to get an article idea out of it.

This activity helps to show members that there are articles to be had everywhere, and it's just a case of looking outside of the box to come up with a unique angle on themes that have been done to death, and grab the attention of editors.

Title Thrillers: Write the most outlandish newspaper headlines you can think of and members have to write a short newspaper article to go with it. You could also search the newspapers for headlines, cut them out and ask members to come up with the news story behind the headline.

The idea behind this is to get members to think about how headlines and titles grab readers' attention and compel them to read on. It helps members to think more carefully about the titles they use in their own writing.

Tickle My Funny Bone: Bring along a selection of jokes and ask members to read them out. Explore if they are funny and if not, why not, if they are, why? Can they make up their own jokes?

This activity not only provides a welcome comic relief to a potentially otherwise dry meeting, it also engages members in the concepts behind comic writing and how to introduce effective comedy into their own writing.

Tour It: Go to a local area of interest and have a guided tour – watch the writing ideas flow. Stately homes, historical places of interest, local landmarks – there's inspiration to be had everywhere.

All Change: have a change of venue – have your meeting outside, in a forest, up a hill, in a swimming pool, in a haunted house at night, etc., and see what happens!

A change is as good as a rest and sometimes we can get too cosy in our boxes and our writing becomes boring, leading to inertia – not a good state for a writer or writing group to get themselves in! Getting out and about reopens your writer's eyes and the inspiration soon starts to gush out of your pen or computer keyboard.

Musical Marbles: Place five cards, each with a different type of music, on the floor in an arc and blindfold members and ask them to roll a marble towards the cards. Whichever one their marble lands on is the type of music they will be writing lyrics for! Bring instrumental examples of the types of music for inspiration too.

Not only is this a lot of fun, it helps members to realise that they can write whatever they want and aren't tied to just one or two styles or genres. It's also about getting to recognise that rhythms and rhymes are best explored through music where you can hear and feel the beat.

Character Chatter: Make some cards with a character type and trait on them and ask members to adopt that character and trait and indulge in some role play with a member with a different character and trait – each member has to guess who the other member's characters and traits are.

This helps members to think about different characters more closely, by 'being' that character and observing other characters, you can make your own characters in your writing more real and three dimensional.

Guess Who?: Attach a card with the name of a famous writer on it onto each member's back. The aim is for members to walk around and ask closed questions until they can work out who they are.

This also works well with famous characters from books or films and is designed to help members improve their interviewing technique by asking questions that get the information they want.

Better Believe It, Baby: Motivational workshop. There's no such word as can't – turn rejection on its head and indulge in a spot of affirmation and positive thinking. Ask members to state as many negative comments about their writing as they can and then turn that negativity into positive comments. For example: 'My character is too weak – they don't seem real,' This turns into, 'My character is weak at the moment, but I can work on her to make her more rounded and believable and give her balance.'

This activity helps members to spot negativity – it can be a sneaky little devil – and learn ways to rewire their negative thoughts to be positive and stop negativity in its tracks.

Appendices

Useful Contacts

For Julie Phillips:

http://writersgrouphandbook.blogspot.com

http://jlpwritersquest.blogspot.com

http://articleangst.blogspot.com

www.facebook.com/writerjuliephillips.

http://thewritewaywritenow.wordpress.com/

NAWG (National Association of Writers' Groups)

www.nawg. co.uk

www.writers-circles.com/links.html

www.hmrc.gov.uk

Writing Magazine https://www.writers-online.co.uk

Writers' Forum www.writers-forum.com

http://authonomy.com

http://youwriteon.com

http://wordpress.com

http://www.myspace.com

http://amazon.co.uk

http://www.smashwords.com

http://www.lulu.com

https://www.createspace.com

http://www.facebook.com

http://www.blogspot.com

http://www.google.com

http://www.yahoo.com

The Writer www.writermag.com/ **(USA)**

Writers' Digest www.writersdigest.com/magazine/ **(USA)**

http://www.irs.gov **(USA)**

**COMPASS
BOOKS**

Compass Books focuses on practical and informative 'how-to'
books for writers. Written by experienced authors who also have
extensive experience of tutoring at the most popular creative
writing workshops, the books offer an insight into the more
specialised niches of the publishing game.